WHEN
HEAVEN
— *IS* —
SILENT

WHEN HEAVEN
IS
SILENT

RONALD DUNN

THOMAS NELSON PUBLISHERS

Nashville

Published in Nashville, Tennessee, by Thomas Nelson, Inc.

All scripture quotations, unless otherwise noted, are taken from the HOLY BIBLE, NEW INTERNATIONAL VERSION ®. Copyright © 1973, 1978, 1984 by International Bible Society. Used by permission of Zondervan Bible Publishing House. All rights reserved.

The "NIV" and "New International Version" trademarks are registered in the United States Patent and Trademark Office by International Bible Society. Use of either trademark requires the permission of International Bible Society.

Scripture quotations noted NAS are from THE NEW AMERICAN STANDARD BIBLE, Copyright © 1960, 1962, 1963, 1968, 1971, 1972, 1973, 1975, 1977 by The Lockman Foundation and are used by permission.

Scripture quotations noted NCV are from The Holy Bible, NEW CENTURY VERSION, Copyright © 1987, 1988, 1991 by Word Publishing Company.

Scripture quotations noted KJV are from The Holy Bible, KING JAMES VERSION.

Library of Congress Cataloging-in-Publication Data

Dunn, Ronald.
  When heaven is silent / Ronald Dunn.
    p. cm.
  Includes bibliographical references.
  ISBN 0-8407-4895-7
1. Suffering—Religious aspects—Christianity.   2. Christian life—
1960–   I. Title.
BT732.7.D857   1994
248.8′6—dc20   94–5604
                                                              CIP

Printed in the United States of America

4 5 6 — 99 98 97 96 95 94

To
KAYE
And Our Three Children
Two Here . . .
STEPHEN MITCHELL
and
KIMBERLY KAYE

And One There . . .
RONALD LOUIS DUNN, JR.
1957–1975
"But our God is in the heavens:
He hath done whatsoever
He hath pleased."

(Psalm 115:3, KJV)

And when he had opened the seventh seal, there was silence in heaven about the space of half an hour.

Revelation 8:1 (KJV)

CONTENTS

ACKNOWLEDGMENTS

No one writes a book alone. From the first word to the last, I have been conscious of many friends, looking over my shoulder, encouraging and supporting and believing. My thanks to:

Dan Benson, who believed in me and this book.

The friends and family who walked with us through the dark and dry times—their love and prayers became an oasis in a desert.

Dr. Ron Hardin, Little Rock, Arkansas, who, like Luke, became a "beloved physician" to me.

Dr. Gary Etter, Irving, Texas, whose skill and understanding helped me through the darkness.

Joanne Gardner, my associate for twenty-seven years, who works hard to make me look good.

My mother-in-law, Eileene Mitchell, who prayed us through many storms.

And my best friend, Kaye, who brought me back from the dead and whose name ought to be on the cover of this book.

BOOK
ONE
TRAVELING IN THE SILENCE

Part One: Preludes

Mark the first page of the book
  With a red marker.
For, in the beginning
  The wound is invisible.
Reb Alce, I Jobes: 13

The God of Israel, the Savior, is sometimes a God that hides Himself but never a God that is absent; sometimes in the dark, but never at a distance.
Matthew Henry

There is nothing to express, nothing with which to express, nothing from which to express, no power to express, no desire to express, together with the obligation to express.
Samuel Beckett

CHAPTER
1

1973: STRANGE MINISTERS

It had been a "honey do" Saturday. You know, "Honey, do this." "Honey, do that"—a day when your procrastination catches up with you and you must pay for your sins. I had spent the day cutting grass, trimming bushes, emptying closets, and cleaning out the garage.

It was around midnight when I finished with the garage. I surveyed my work and decided that ought to hold it for another ten years. As I was heading for the bathroom to take a shower, Kaye asked me to run up to the all-night supermarket to pick up some things for breakfast.

I examined myself in the mirror. Yuck. I hadn't shaved or combed my hair. I was wearing a soiled T-shirt and faded blue jeans with portholes in the knees. My tennis shoes were in the final stages of leprosy. The security guard would probably frisk me before letting me enter the store. Not the image a dignified pastor of the local church wants to project. But, hey, how many people shop for groceries at midnight?

A lot of people shop for groceries at midnight. I discovered a subculture of midnight shoppers. The thing to do, of course, was to grab my few items and get out before anyone I knew spotted me. I kept my head down, looking neither to the left nor to the right.

And then I was standing in line at the check-out with only one person in front of me: a woman from my church. The devil made her turn around and look at me, then turn back, then turn back again, screwing up her eyes, giving me the once-over. And then recognition sprang to her eyes. "Brother Dunn!" she gasped.

I don't know who was more embarrassed. After I mumbled some sort of explanation, she said, "I didn't recognize you without a suit and tie."

As I drove home, I thought about her words: "I didn't recognize you without a suit and tie." I had been her pastor for seven years; she was present every week, Sunday morning and Sunday night. I calculated she had heard *and seen* me preach about seven hundred times—and she didn't recognize me without a suit and tie. What had she been looking at all those years—me or my clothes? If she was driving down the road at night and saw one of my suits and ties on the side of the road, she would probably say, "There's the pastor's suit and tie." But me she wouldn't recognize.

I remembered reading somewhere that the best disguise is a uniform because people look at the uniform, not the person wearing it. I knew this was true.

I recalled sitting with my wife and daughter all night in the Gatwick airport in London, waiting for our flight back to the States. There were about a hundred others in the waiting area. One man, sitting a couple of rows away, kept watching me. When he saw me looking at him looking at me, he rose and walked over.

"Are you from Irving, Texas?" he asked.

"Uh, well, yes, I am."

He grinned and offered his hand. "I'm your postman."

I half-expected him to deliver a letter right then and there. A few days later I stood beside my mailbox and waited for my postman, and sure enough, it was him. All I had seen before was the uniform.

I didn't recognize my postman in London because he was out of uniform and didn't look like a postman. That church member didn't recognize her minister because he was out of uniform and didn't look like a minister.

The thought pounded at me: How many ministers had I missed because they didn't look like ministers? How many blessings had I forfeited because they looked like curses? How many kings had I turned away from my door because they were clad in the rags of a beggar?

As I thought about it I realized that some of the greatest ministers God had sent to me were "strange ministers"—out of uniform and out of the pulpit—and I didn't recognize them because they didn't look the way ministers are supposed to look.

CHAPTER

2

1975: THE STRANGEST MINISTER

The December sky was the color of tarnished silver, as was the casket that stood a few feet away in front of the family and friends gathered under the tent at the graveside. A close friend of the family was speaking.

"There can be no final explanation for Ronnie, Jr.'s death, and the chances are if there were human explanations they would not yield as much benefit as we are all experiencing. The fact that we cannot explain it gives the whole experience more awe and respect.

"There will likely be no life which has had or will have as much effect for good and growth in all your lives than that of Ronnie, Jr. There will be no circumstance that will contribute more to your spiritual deepening than this one. What the Bible says of Samson will be true of Ronnie, Jr.: 'He slew more Philistines in his death than he did in all his life.' Ronnie, Jr.'s life and death will have immeasurable influence on you until Jesus comes or we go.

"He is closer to all of you right now than he ever has been before. You sense his presence as you never have.

You fellowship with him through Jesus as you never did ... even in the best of times. He is whole. He understands. He loves.

"We all know that Ron has a series of messages called 'Strange Ministers.' Today we are being ministered to by the strangest minister of all—death."

CHAPTER

3

THE PRESENT: A MEMO TO THE READER

I'm writing this book in self-defense. Now that I think about it, most of my preaching these past few years has been in self-defense, preaching to answer my own questions, to defend myself against the assault of conflicting truths, the disparity between belief and experience.

Perhaps you know what I mean. I'm talking about those times when you have every board nailed down, every cover tucked in—you know what you believe, and it all makes sense. And then comes the jarring note—you are suddenly faced with equally true but contrary facts. And if your faith is to survive, you must somehow reconcile two indisputable, but opposing, ideas. As one said, "My ontological security was at stake."[1]

There's a word for this: *dissonance*. Dissonance is "the rough, harsh and unpleasant effect of two tones sounded simultaneously which do not blend or fuse, attributed to *beats* which are too rapid to be separately distinguished."[2]

Dissonance is discord, incongruity, a lack of harmony. Psychologists have a term for it. They call it "cognitive dissonance." That's when there is dissonance and *you know it*. It rattles your teeth and bursts your eardrums. You have dissonance, and you are cognitive of it. The task, of course, is to get rid of the discord. To accomplish this we may change our beliefs or distort reality to fit those beliefs. "Studies show that worshippers do not surrender their beliefs in the face of disconfirming facts. They simply adjust their beliefs to neutralize the facts."[3]

Right now I'm up to my eyeballs in cognitive dissonance. To tell you the truth, I thought all my strange ministers were behind me. I've had my share; I've paid my dues. I thought I deserved an "all clear" signal; instead, I got a "storm warning."

The day I sat down to write, a new crisis barged into our lives. Suddenly, the last thing I wanted to do was write, or even think about "strange ministers" and the silence of heaven.

So I am writing this as much for me as for you. Oh, one other thing about dissonance: In music, dissonance is a chord that sounds harsh and incomplete until resolved to a harmonious chord. I'm looking for that chord. And I will tell you the truth about what I find.

Honest.

I promise.

Part Two: Wrestling with the Angel

As long as we want to be different from what God wants us to be at the time, we are only tormenting ourselves to no purpose.

Gerhart Tersteegen

The things for which we visit a man were done alone in the dark and the cold.

Henry David Thoreau

But how can God bring this about in me?—Let Him do it and perhaps you will know.

George MacDonald

CHAPTER

4

THE OTHER SIDE OF THE ABUNDANT LIFE

"Can't you just give me a pill?"

The doctor looked up from his notepad and smiled, shaking his head. He thought I was joking. I wasn't.

Shot was what I was. Shot, run down, burned out, depressed—whatever you want to call it. Life in the fast-food lane had caught up with me. Ten years of itinerant ministry, overloaded schedules, hundreds of monotonous motel rooms and fast food restaurants had taken their toll. On my way to saving the world, I had acquired a stomach disorder that was throwing me into the hospital with increasing frequency, threatening my ministry and my sanity. I had lost thirty pounds and felt as bad as I looked—which was why I was in the doctor's office.

He had concluded that my problems were caused by the accumulated stress of a decade of "overdoing it." My stomach has more sense than my head, he said. A return to normalcy was what I needed, he said.

He picked up a notepad and began writing. "I'm going to give you a list of things you need to start doing right now," he said. "First, I want you to walk three miles a day, four days a week. And do it in forty-five minutes. No lallygagging out there.

"Second," he said, "I want you to eat at least two nutritious, well-balanced meals every day.

"Third, plan to get seven to eight hours of sleep every night. And remember, the hours before midnight are the best."

That's when I said, "Can't you just give me a pill or something?"

To tell you the truth, I wasn't interested in walking three miles a day, four days a week; and with my schedule, there was no way to get seven or eight hours of sleep at night. And before midnight—forget it. And have you ever tried to maintain a nutritious, well-balanced diet eating church lunches, frozen fast food, and motel mystery meals? To me a well-balanced meal was a Coke in one hand and a pepperoni pizza in the other.

I was too busy to get well. I wanted to get well—but without changing my lifestyle. Discipline can be extremely inconvenient. I wanted a pill. The doctor assured me there was no such pill, but I'm still looking. If you hear of anything. . . .

I am not alone in my quest for the quick-fix. The doctors I talk to say that most of their patients come to them looking for a way to continue living as they like, but without suffering the consequences. I remember what Dr. Paul Tournier wrote about a patient consulting a doctor:

> What he is looking for is a medicine that will make it unnecessary for him to change his life, so that he can go on living in accordance with his whims and passions, count-

ing on some wonder-working pill to rescue him from their awkward circumstances.[1]

We look for the easy path, always ripe for a quick-fix scheme. Instant gratification is the order of the day.

Unfortunately, we approach the Christian life with the same attitude. We desperately want to believe that all our problems can be solved if we can just find the right button to push. Maybe we'll find the secret at the next seminar. Perhaps this set of tapes will do the trick, this book, this preacher.

And speaking of preachers, I reckon we are largely to blame for our hearers' thinking this way. We like to preach about the victorious life—and people like to hear about it. It seems right that the good news of Christ should offer a life of overcoming and abundance—and it does. The problem is that we have stated it one way and our listeners have interpreted it another.

We tell stories about people like D. L. Moody, who was so overcome by the power of God on a New York street he had to seek refuge in his room. As wave after wave of the love of God washed over him, he had to ask God, "Stay Thy hand!"

"I went to preaching again," Moody says. "The sermons were the same; I did not present any new truth. Yet hundreds were converted."

"Yes!" we cry. "That's it! That's what I need! That's what I'm seeking!"

The story is true, but not all the truth. We never know the whole story. People have a secret history with God—and we can never read the pages of a person's secret history. We see them on the mountaintop, but we do not know of the climb to the top, or of the descent into the valley.

Ironically, looking for an experience that will set us free puts us in bondage. The keepers of this prison demand of me an instant cure, all my problems solved in one fell swoop. They will not allow me to grow gradually, bit by bit. They have no patience with that sort of thing. You must be changed now! Instantly! Completely! They insist I leap from adolescence to adulthood in one day, that all the problems of living be settled in one blazing experience.

The result? Guilt. *What's wrong with me?*

A DOSE OF REALITY WOULD HELP

During our lifetime we write two books. The first is the Book of Dreams. We write this book when we are young, when our life stretches before us and we can't wait to get there. It is packed with excitement, adventure, and romance; it is filled with anticipation, a prophecy of everything we want to be and do.

We write the second book as we catch up with our future. This is the book of what we really become and really accomplish. This is the Book of Reality—and any similarity between the two is purely coincidental. From the beginning God has caught me off-guard, kept me off balance, taken me by surprise. He has not worked as I expected. His style has frustrated me. At many junctures in my life I have had to confess with Jacob, "Surely the LORD is in this place, and I was not aware of it" (Gen. 28:16). Just about the time I think I have it all together, it all comes apart.

Enter Jacob. His story has helped me to understand how God deals with His servants, how He makes them what He wants them to be. This is especially true of Jacob's bizarre encounter with the stranger by the River Jabbok, recorded in Genesis 32. It is a paradigm of God's methods. Nowhere in the Bible will we find a better example of how God uses strange ministers to conform us to the image of His Son.

If you don't know Jacob, let me introduce him by telling you the meaning of his name and how he got it.

ALL MY SONS

From the first scene until the final curtain, Jacob's story reads like an episode from a soap opera. The cast of characters are Isaac, the father; Rebekah, the mother; and Esau and Jacob, twin brothers.

The twins were an answer to prayer. Their mother, Rebekah, was barren, which was a mark of reproach to the Hebrews, and Isaac "prayed to the LORD on behalf of his wife, because she was barren. The LORD answered his prayer and his wife Rebekah became pregnant" (Gen. 25:21).

But there was trouble from the start. "The children struggled together within her" (Gen. 25:22, KJV). The two brothers were fighting even before they were born—in the womb. The struggle between them was so fierce that Rebekah cried out to God in despair. If the life she was carrying was truly a gift from God, a miraculous answer to prayer, why this struggle? She couldn't reconcile the blessing and the battle.

And God answered her: "Two nations are in your womb, and two peoples from within you will be separated; one people will be stronger than the other, and the older will serve the younger" (Gen. 25:23). The older will serve the younger? That spells trouble.

The big day came. Esau emerged from the womb first—the elder brother. Because he was red and covered with hair, they named him Esau, which means "hairy." Jacob followed swiftly, coming from the womb with his hand grasping Esau's heel, so they named him Jacob, which means "heel-catcher."

And the name was perfect for the person. The Hebrew word for "Jacob" casts a strong image. It means to seize by the heel, to trip someone by grabbing the heel. The word reeks with deceit. It's a sneak attack. It describes someone who lies in wait to ambush an enemy. Fraudulent, deceitful, crooked—this is the character of a "Jacob." (And this is the one God chose to love!) When Jeremiah the prophet says that "the heart is deceitful above all things," he uses the same word—"the heart is a *Jacob*" (Jer. 17:9, KJV).

And Jacob lived up to his name. Having first maneuvered Esau out of his birthright, he then tricked his blind and dying father into giving him the blessing that belonged to Esau, the older brother. When Esau learned he had lost the blessing, he cried out: "Isn't he rightly named Jacob? . . . He took my birthright, and now he's taken my blessing!" (Gen. 27:36).

Esau vowed that as soon as the mourning period for his father's death had passed he would kill his brother. Discretion being the better part of valour, Jacob took his mother's advice to visit his Uncle Laban in Haran.

That had been twenty years earlier.

Now Jacob was returning home.

And Esau was riding to meet him with four hundred men.

Jacob immediately divided his camp into two groups so that if Esau attacked one group, the other could escape.

Then he sent a huge bribe to Esau. You get an idea of how wealthy Jacob had become by the size of the bribe: 200 female goats, 20 male goats, 200 ewes, 20 rams, 30 female camels with their young, 40 cows, 10 bulls, 20 female donkeys, and 10 male donkeys.

When night fell, Jacob sent his two wives, Rachel and Leah; his eleven sons; and two maidservants across the ford of the Jabbok. Afterward he sent over all his possessions.

Having already pleaded with God to save him from Esau, there was nothing to do now but wait. Or so he thought.

> So Jacob was left alone, and a man wrestled with him till daybreak. When the man saw that he could not overpower him, he touched the socket of Jacob's hip so that his hip was wrenched as he wrestled with the man. Then the man said, "Let me go, for it is daybreak."
> But Jacob replied, "I will not let you go unless you bless me."
> The man asked him, "What is your name?"
> "Jacob," he answered.
> Then the man said, "Your name will no longer be Jacob, but Israel, because you have struggled with God and with men and have overcome."
> Jacob said, "Please tell me your name."
> But he replied, "Why do you ask my name?" Then he blessed him there.
> So Jacob called the place Peniel, saying, "It is because I saw God face to face, and yet my life was spared."
> The sun rose above him as he passed Peniel, and he was limping because of his hip. Therefore to this day the Israelites do not eat the tendon attached to the socket of the hip, because the socket of Jacob's hip was touched near the tendon. (Gen. 32:24–32)

That this strange story held special significance for the Israelites is evidenced by three things: (1) Jacob is given a new name—Israel; (2) the name given to the site—Peniel, "the face of God"; (3) the cultic ban on eating the tendon attached to the hip.

The significance? Here is a picture of how God deals with His people. This is how God makes an Israel out of a

Jacob. This is how God makes a prince out of a con man. This is how God takes us as we are and makes us what we should be.

And—are you ready for this?—*it is a struggle until the breaking of the day.*

CHAPTER
5

OUR TOUGHEST BATTLES ARE WITH GOD

Let's set the scene. Jacob is alone in the dark, waiting, wondering, worrying. What will happen tomorrow? Will his brother accept his gifts (bribe) or kill him? He's uptight, on edge, anxious.

Suddenly, without warning, a "man" leaps out of the darkness and wrestles Jacob to the ground.

Now who do you suppose Jacob thought that was? Esau? That must have been his first thought. Esau has taken a page out of Jacob's book and launched a sneak attack.

Or perhaps it was one of Esau's men, an expert in silent assassination. Or a thug who just happened to pass by and seized the opportunity to mug a tourist.

Or maybe Jacob thought it was a river demon trying to prevent him from crossing the river. Many people believed in those things—like the local sheriff trying to keep the riffraff out of his town.

Or maybe, as the ancient rabbis suggested, it was Jacob's guardian angel![1] I like that—imagine Jacob, so despicable a character that the very angel assigned to guard him attacks him.

Or who knows? I don't know who Jacob thought it was, but I know who Jacob thought it *was not*. He didn't think, "Oh, joy, a friend has come to bless me!"

He didn't think that it was God, because he had asked God to save him. No, only someone with evil intentions would do this. This was not the greeting of a benefactor; this was the aggression of an enemy.

And then.

Somehow, some way, Jacob, in a flash of revelation, saw the truth: His unknown assailant was—Genesis says "man"; Hosea 12 says "angel"—but in whatever form, we know it was God.

Jacob had prayed for protection from Esau; what he needed was protection from God. Esau was not his problem—God was his problem.

What a revelation! And what a revolution it wrought in Jacob, because, seen from this perspective, all our battles and conflicts take on new meaning. Enemies are turned into servants. Monsters become ministers. "We do not always recognize it as God. He appears in the form, or force, of restlessness, as he did with Jacob. But in some moments He appears as God. The unknown force in us that caused our restlessness becomes manifest as the God in whose hands we are, Who is our ultimate threat and our ultimate refuge."[2]

Our toughest battles are with God, not the devil. I'm not denying the reality of spiritual warfare with satanic powers. I am only saying that I find it *easier to say no to the devil than to say yes to God*.

For examples of this, we don't have to dig into the dusty corners of the Bible and drag out obscure bit players.

Remember Abraham? When God said He was bypassing Ishmael in favor of Isaac, Abraham cried out, "O, that Ishmael might live before You!" (Gen. 17:18). His controversy was with God, not the devil.

What about Job? This veteran makes guest appearances in every book on suffering—and this one is no exception. In Job's story, Satan disappears after the second chapter, never to be heard from again. Actually, Satan plays a minor role in the story. He is the tool of providence. While the devil inflicted the pain, it was God who started the whole affair by drawing attention to Job's unequaled character. Job himself never mentions Satan, much less give him credit for what happened. As Augustine observed, Job did not say, "The Lord gave and the *Devil* hath taken away."

The book of Job is not a story about passive submission; it is a story of active protest, and protest directed to God. Job's battle is with God, not with the devil.

Jeremiah is called the "weeping prophet"—and for good reason. For more than forty years he faithfully proclaimed a harsh and bitter message from God to his countrymen. Before Jeremiah was formed in the womb, God bestowed upon this priest's son from Anathoth the office of prophet.

At first everything was great. He speaks to the Lord, "When your words came, I ate them; they were my joy and my heart's delight" (Jer. 15:16). But then things turned sour. As an object lesson to Judah, Jeremiah was not allowed to marry. Because of his message he was ostracized by his countrymen and threatened with death in his hometown. He was thrown into prison, tried for his life by the priests and prophets of Jerusalem, locked in stocks, publicly humiliated, and thrown into a cistern.

Heartbroken, this lonely prophet brings his complaints to the Lord, seeking some understanding and relief. How does God respond? Listen.

"If you have raced with men on foot and they have worn you out, how can you compete with horses? If you stumble in safe country, how will you manage in the thickets by the Jordan?" (Jer. 12:5).

Don't be such a cry-baby, Jeremiah. You think this is bad? It's going to get worse. You want to quit? You haven't even started.

Jeremiah's greatest struggles were not with the stiff-necked people who rejected his message and wanted to kill him; his greatest struggle was with the God who had called him.

Mention could be made of another prophet, Habakkuk, whose little book bearing his name deals almost exclusively with the prophet's impassioned protests to God for allowing the wicked to go unpunished, and then because of the way God did punish the wicked.

And then there is Jesus—I hesitate to walk on this holy ground. His struggle in the Garden of Gethsemane on the eve of His crucifixion is beyond telling. We have only a handful of words that hint at His agony. Having told His disciples that His soul was in agony to the point of dying . . .

> He went a little farther and fell on His face, and prayed, saying, "O My Father, if it is possible, let this cup pass from Me; nevertheless, not as I will but as You will. (Matt. 26:39)

> Three times Jesus repeated His prayer. Then an angel appeared to Him from heaven, strengthening Him. And being in agony He prayed more earnestly. And His sweat became like great drops of blood falling down to the ground. (Luke 22:43–44)

At the beginning of His ministry, Jesus fasted forty days and nights in the wilderness, and then in a physically weakened condition, He wrestled with the Tempter. We cannot know the severity of that battle, but we do know that when Jesus wrestled with the devil in the wilderness, He did not sweat blood.

And who can measure the horrifying, agonizing wail from the cross: "My God, My God, Why have You forsaken Me?"

WHAT IS YOUR NAME?

Why is the struggle so relentless? Because God wants to change us, and we don't want to be changed. Not really, not the kind of change God wants. I mean *really* change. Not cosmetic surgery, but radical surgery—that's what God's after. He intends to reach down into the guts of our soul and rip the Jacob out of us.

Why do you suppose the angel asked for Jacob's name? Was he gathering information? Had God sent him with an arrest warrant made out "To whom it may concern"? I doubt it.

Confession—that's what the angel sought. Not information, but confession. In the Hebrew, if the question is of one's identity, it is phrased, "Who are you?" But "What is your name?" is another matter. That question deals with the character of the person, the meaning of his name.

Do you want the blessing? How badly? What is your name, your real name, down in the darkest depths, in the hidden labyrinths of your being?

God was forcing Jacob to face the truth about himself, and that's always a fight. As T. S. Eliot said, man cannot take too much truth at one time, especially truth about himself. Our capacity for self-deception is gargantuan; it is how we survive.

"Say it! There is no other way. You will never understand your life until you understand your name."

And he cried out, "Jacob!" No, he cried out, "Fraud! Cheat! Deceiver! Swindler!"

What would you answer? What would I? We'd rather not think about it.

THE SECOND TIME AROUND

This is not Jacob's first dramatic encounter with God. Twenty years before there had been another. At Bethel. His first night on the lam. That night as he slept, he had a dream, and a magnificent dream it was. He saw a ladder reaching from heaven to earth with angels ascending and descending upon it, and standing above was the Lord, who spoke to Jacob, promising that He would be with him wherever he went and that one day He would bring Jacob back home (Gen. 28:10–22).

Now that's what I call an experience! I'll tell you how powerful it was: Jacob signed a pledge card right then and there, pledging to tithe everything he had. That's the kind of experience I need. God, show me some angels, and I'll be okay; let me see some angels, and I'll change; give me a vision, and I'll become a new person. Can you imagine what that kind of an experience would do to your Christian life?

But here he is twenty years later, still the same old Jacob.

It's scary how many great experiences we can have and remain unchanged.

And now he's about to meet God again. But this encounter is going to be different. The first one had been thrilling and ecstatic; this one is going to be frightening and painful. But Jacob will not walk away from this meeting unchanged. He will limp away, transformed, a prince. The secret of victory is losing the right battle.

FROM PIMPLES TO TUMORS

As we grow older our battles with God grow more fierce, even more painful at times. The issues are more critical, the outcomes more profound.

When I was a teenager I was positively, absolutely certain that as I grew older my spiritual battles would be easier, and eventually eliminated. That's what I thought at sixteen; that's what I thought at twenty; that's what I thought at thirty and forty and fifty. Today I wish the only things I had to worry about now were the things I worried about when I was sixteen. Back then God was after pimples. Now He's after tumors.

There is no single, once for all, life-changing event. We do not solve the problems of life in a single day. The great decisions of life are not made suddenly in a thirty-second experience at a church altar. They are made gradually, over a period of time, when we are alone in the dark.

That's how God met Jacob. Remember, the overwhelming picture in this story is that of God as the *Aggressor*. Like a cunning thief, the "man" plans his attack to catch his victim off guard and defenseless. He waits until "Jacob was left alone," with no one to help or rescue him. The whole story reads like a script, care given to each detail, even to the play on words—Jacob wrestling at Jabbok—all of it according to plan.

He was alone. And so are we, alone with God. It always comes down to this—just God and me.

It was dark, and Jacob could not identify his attacker. And so it is with us. We know we are wrestling, but with whom we can't be certain—God? Satan? Ourselves?

The struggle is inescapable. Jacob has no choice; he must fight. The sort of fight the Aggressor chooses is significant—wrestling. If someone punches you in the nose and you don't want to fight, you can run away. But if someone leaps on you, wraps his arms around you, and throws you to the ground, you are going to fight, like it or not. You have no choice. The struggle is inescapable.

Jacob had been running for twenty years, but now God overtakes him, seals him off, and isolates him. And now Jacob must face God—and himself.

This is the truth about all of us. We flee the presence of God, even while we serve Him. We speak to Him but avoid His eyes lest they penetrate our defenses and we are exposed. But God pursues and overtakes us; He arrests us only to bless us.

A friend once commented to me how much he admired my dedication and commitment to God. I tried to tell him the truth, but he didn't understand. As I survey my experience, I do not see any voluntary submission to God, no noble sacrifice for the heroic thing. Rather, I am more aware of being acted upon, rather than acting, of being chosen rather than choosing, of being drafted rather than volunteering. Whatever my submission, it was a "say uncle" situation to me. God pursued me and wore me down until, exhausted, I cried, "Uncle," or was it "Jacob"? I know we must allow for man's choice and responsibility; all I'm saying is that my feeling is not one of noble sacrifice. In my mind I see God dragging me every step of the way with me kicking and screaming.

I know myself too well. At the bottom, I am a rebel, and if God left me to myself I would run away.

But what is most amazing about this is that it gives me a deep peace because I know God has set His love on me, and that whatever my hardheadedness, He will not abandon me to myself. He will pursue me with a stubborn love that will not let me go.

Also there is confidence that where I am, I am there because He maneuvered me there. I have great assurance that hither by His grace I've come. His grace has brought me safe thus far, and grace will lead me home. I wish I could say the initiative was mine, that mine has always been the glad surrender. I honestly tried—a few times—but I ran out of resolve, out of commitment, out of love. But I did not run out of Him.

CHAPTER

6

THROWING AWAY
OUR BLESSINGS

It was right across the street from our motel in Mississippi: the perfect house for an antique shop—large, two-storied, white frame with an antebellum face, sheltered by ancient trees. When Kaye and I stepped onto the veranda, I smelled magnolia blossoms and saw General Robert E. Lee sitting in a rocking chair, sipping a mint julep.

As we made our way through the thicket of tables laden with antiques of all sizes and shapes, I picked up several, glanced at the price tags, and carefully returned them to their resting place. I kept thinking, "I've thrown away better stuff than this!"

For years, I've looked for the baseball card collection I had when I was a kid. I started saving them in 1948—Hank Greenberg, Bob Feller, Mickey Mantle. Do you know how much those cards are worth today? I kept them in my Cub Scout scrapbook. But I can't find them anywhere. My mother died before I realized how valuable they were, so it was too late to ask her. I hate to think about what must have happened—Mom threw them away when I went off to college. But how was I to know that Mickey Mantle's rookie card would someday be worth thousands of dollars?

I can't believe that I sold my '65 Mustang for $400! But who would have imagined that it would be worth ten times that now? I'm telling my children: Don't throw away *anything!* Save it all; buy a storage garage if you have to, but don't throw stuff away.

My problem is that I can't always tell the difference between treasure and trash. Through the years I have thrown away a lot of treasures because at the time they looked like trash. We all have.

And we will probably continue to do so, because we are positive we can tell the difference. After all, I know trash when I see it. I know a curse when I see one, and I know a blessing when I see one. Are you trying to tell me *this* is a blessing? Hah! This is definitely a curse, and I'm getting rid of it as soon as I can.

You see, we humans have a fatal flaw: We believe we can accurately interpret every event and experience in our lives. But kings sometimes come to our door dressed as beggars, and blessings as curses, and we often entertain angels unaware.

It would be nice if we could see ahead and know what to save and what to throw away, what is trash and what is treasure, and what junk will become antiques. But . . .

JACOB'S HARD LESSON

I am reluctant to say this because it is something I'd rather not hear and something I do not want to acknowledge, but *the greatest works God has done in my life, He has done against my pleasure—and against my will.* We wrestle against the very things God sends to bless us. Like Jacob, we often try to throw away our blessings.

But sometimes, like Jacob, we see junk turn into antiques right before our eyes, even as we struggle against it.

As we saw in the last chapter, God had Jacob right where He wanted him. Jacob was alone—there was no one to rescue him. He was in the grasp of an unknown assailant; there was no escape.

Jacob was fighting for his life, struggling to break the hold of his enemy, when suddenly everything changed. Now it's the attacker who is trying to get loose and Jacob who is grasping. "I will not let you go unless you bless me," he said. Jacob realized that he was not wrestling with a curse, as he first thought, but with a blessing.

And this is one of the most remarkable things about the whole adventure: What Jacob at first sought to escape, he now embraces; the thing he tried to throw down, he now clings to. This is how God transforms a Jacob into an Israel.

And so I repeat: *The very thing I'm wrestling against may be the thing God wants to use to bless me.*

RETREAT FROM REALITY

I am learning that faith is more than the power to change things for the better. Oh, we would like to do that. But that isn't faith's greatest power.

Speaking of power, we *are* obsessed with it. Popular spirituality is power-based; everything is interpreted in terms of power. Today's religion is Power Religion, filled with power language and power images. In his forceful book *God and Human Suffering*, Douglas John Hall quotes Kosuke Koyama:

The name, Jesus Christ, is not a magic name which transforms the broken world into an instant paradise. Has not the true dimension of the glory of this name suffered since the faith associated with this name became the state religion of the Roman Empire? Has it not been difficult to maintain the quality of the stumbling block of this name when the church became the powerful social group? How could the prestigious church proclaim the crucified Christ? The name of Jesus Christ is not a powerful name in the manner of imperial power. It is a "foolish and weak" name (I Cor. 1:21–25)! . . . Jesus Christ is not a quick answer. If Jesus Christ is the answer he is the answer in the way portrayed in the crucifixion.[1]

Hall goes on to say that "the church . . . has permitted its message to be filtered through the sieve of worldly power and glory."[2] In our attempt to win the world by impressing the world, we have abandoned the confrontational language of the cross for the wooing language of power, might, success, and winning. The true power of our faith is power that the world calls weakness, and the victory of our faith is victory that the world calls failure.[3]

The Christ we profess to follow was made "perfect through suffering" (Heb. 2:10). We prefer to be made perfect through success. But grace will not do for us what it did not do for Christ—exempt us from suffering.

"THAT'S A POOR SALES PITCH"

Jesus was brutally honest. He never left His followers in doubt as to what awaited them; He did not dazzle them with promises of riches and honor and power. Rather, He spoke of carrying a cross and denying self, of persecution and ridicule, of losing in order to find, of dying in order to live. In short, He never promised them a rose garden.

Let's listen to Jesus as He renews His call to Simon Peter in John 21. The resurrected Lord has dined with his disciples on bread and fish that He Himself prepared. After dinner Jesus invites Peter to take a walk with Him. As they walk, Jesus suddenly says, "Simon son of John, do you truly love me more than these?" (v. 15).

And Peter answers, "'Yes, Lord. . . . You know that I love you.'"

Jesus said, "Feed my lambs'" (v. 15).

This is done three times and then Jesus gets to the bottom line: "'I tell you the truth,'" He says to Peter, "'when you were younger you dressed yourself and went where you wanted; but when you are old you will stretch out your hands, and someone else will dress you and lead you to where you do not want to go'" (v. 18).

He said this, John tells us, "to indicate the kind of death by which Peter would glorify God" (v. 19).

And then, after describing what will happen if Peter follows Jesus, the Lord says, "Follow me!"

I wrote in the margin of my Bible, "That's a poor sales pitch and bad psychology."

Jesus could have said, "Peter, if you follow me you will become famous, you will preach the Pentecostal sermon, you'll write part of the Bible, and a lot of people will call you the first pope." Now that's a sales pitch.

But the only thing Jesus promised was a martyr's death.

Several years ago my denomination revised its hymnbook, putting in some new songs and taking out some old ones. And they took out one of my all-time favorites: "Jesus, I My Cross Have Taken." Are you familiar with it? The first verse goes like this:

> Jesus, I my cross have taken,
>   All to leave and follow Thee;
> Destitute, despised, forsaken,
>   Thou from hence my all shalt be:
> Perish every fond ambition,
>   All I've sought, and hoped and known;
> Yet how rich is my condition,
>   God and heav'n are still my own.

And it has other verses, too, with phrases like, "Let the world despise and leave me," and "Foes may hate and friends may shun me."

I sought out a member of the review board and asked him why they removed that hymn. His answer?

"We felt that it portrayed a poor self-image and might contribute to a low self-esteem."

In other words, it's bad psychology.

ESCAPE OR ENDURE?

We're big on escaping but not much on enduring. Well, of course we're not. Who wants to endure when you can escape? Propelled by that very natural feeling we have tried to turn Christianity into a religion of escape. But as a follower of Jesus I must remember that He chose to endure rather than escape. He could have escaped but didn't; we can't, but we die trying. And the more we anticipate escaping, the less strength we have to endure.

And so I say that faith is not necessarily the power to make things the way we want them to be; it is the courage to face things as they are.

Remember when the disciples and a sleeping Jesus ran into a storm on the sea? (Mark 4:35–41). They shook Jesus awake, crying, "Teacher, don't you care if we drown?" Jesus awoke and did two things: He stilled the storm and rebuked the disciples for their lack of faith. But He didn't rebuke them because they didn't have enough faith to still the storm. He rebuked them for not having enough faith to stay calm in the storm—especially with Jesus on board.

Now I want to make it clear that I'm not advocating passive resignation. If I can change things for the better, I should. If I have a headache, I'll take an aspirin. Resignation means that I give up, enclosing myself in a shell of self-pity, unable to see any purpose for my condition, powerless to extract any good from it. I give up on life, fearing it more than death.

As far as finding meaning in suffering is concerned, Viktor Frankl notes that it only has meaning "provided . . . that the suffering is unavoidable. If it is avoidable, the meaningful thing to do is to remove its cause, for unnecessary suffering is masochistic rather than heroic. If, on the other hand, one cannot change a situation that causes his suffering, he can still choose his attitude."[4]

"I HAVE SEEN GOD FACE TO FACE."

When Jacob limped away the next morning, he named the place of his dark encounter Peniel—"It is because I saw God face to face, and yet my life was spared." He could have named the spot "The Place of Struggle" or "The Place of Pain" or something similar—and it would have been correct, for so it was. Sometimes we do give our times of wrestlings names like that—which, I guess, says a lot about us.

We can only call those dark encounters Peniel when we realize that faith is:

- the wisdom to see treasure in trash;
- the courage to face things as they are, not as we wish them to be;

- the boldness to embrace those things and say, "I will not let you go unless you bless me," making our greatest weakness our greatest strength.

Then, and only then, do these "things" become fuel for our journey and construction material for building a Christ-like life.

CHAPTER

7

GOOD AND BAD RUN ON PARALLEL TRACKS, AND THEY USUALLY ARRIVE AT THE SAME TIME

"I will not let you go until you bless me!"

This is the cry of a disabled man, disabled by the blow of an angel, disabled yet clinging to his attacker. It is the cry of a desperate man who, in spite of the pain, refuses to loosen his grip on the angel until the angel loosens his grip on the blessing Jacob seeks. For all such desperate seekers of the Lord's face, the outcome is, "And he blessed him there."

There are two noteworthy points about this blessing. First, this is the only place in the Bible where a blessing was obtained through a struggle. You didn't get blessings by struggling for them; they were conferred upon you.

But this blessing Jacob had to fight for. It was the first time he ever had to fight for anything. He always used his

41

wits, his cleverness, his deceit. Jacob was a con man. But he couldn't con the angel. This time he had to struggle.

Second, the word *blessed* here means "a transfer of power." The angel blessed him there—that means the angel transferred his power to Jacob. Think of it—*the power of an angel.*

But at the same time the angel gave him the power, he also popped Jacob on the hip and gave him a limp he would struggle with the rest of his life.

Jacob came away with what he wanted, and with what he didn't want. It was good and bad running on parallel tracks and arriving at the same time.

IS THIS A REHEARSAL OR THE REAL THING?

For a long time I had a distorted view of life. I would look at my life and think that there are some good things going on, but there are also a lot of bad things. There's some good stuff coming down the pike, but there's some bad stuff, too. And I know that's not how it's supposed to be. I'll just pull over here on the side and wait it out, and one of these days I'll get it all together and then nothing but good things will happen—which is the way life is supposed to be lived. Right?

Don't tell me you haven't at times tried to put off your life. Put it on hold? Till you finish school. Till the kids are grown. Till you complete your apprenticeship and land the big job.

Most of us live our lives as though we were rehearsing for the real thing. But as someone said, "Life is what happens while you're waiting for life to start."

We idealize life, reasoning that if God is really working in our lives, nothing but good will come down. But as Lewis Smedes says, "Keep in mind that we are always grateful for one thing in spite of something else. Every silver lining must have a cloud."[1]

THE MYSTERY OF GOOD AND EVIL

Do you remember Jesus' parable of the wheat and the tares? (Matt. 13:24–30, 36–43). A man sowed good seed in his field, and during the night an enemy sowed tares among the wheat. When the servants realized what had happened they suggested to their master the only sensible response: "Do you want us to go and pull them up?" Of course! we would say. That is the only rational course of action.

But the master surprises us all when he replies, "No, because while you are pulling up the tares, you may root up the wheat with them. Let both grow together until the harvest."

Jesus is addressing one of the greatest mysteries of life: the mystery of good and evil. When the servants saw what had happened they said, "Sir, didn't you sow good seed in your field? Where did these tares come from?"

And that has been the despairing cry of us all: "Where did this evil come from? I sowed good seed in my life and in my home and in my children. Where did all these heartaches and disappointments come from? Why is my life choked with evil?"

And even more despairing is the cry, "And why doesn't the Lord weed out the evil? Why does He allow evil to live in the world and intertwine itself into every relation of life?"

The real mystery of good and evil is the *mixture* of good and evil. That's the mystery; they are *mixed*. And that's the point of Jesus' parable.

THERE IS A JUDGMENT BEYOND
OUR JUDGMENT

"Let them grow together," Jesus says. During the night an enemy sowed tares among the wheat. "Among the wheat" is a strong Greek expression meaning "all through the midst of the wheat, between and on top of." The roots had become so inextricably intertwined that any attempt to pull them out would have torn out the wheat also. You can't root out the bad without rooting out the good. Wait until harvest when they will all be rooted out, then separate the good from the bad.

The tares do not worry the Master. He will take care of them in due time. Make no mistake about it, God's control is never usurped. He is in sovereign control. It is *His* field, and He will tend it properly.

Now frankly, I'm a little nervous about saying this, but it seems that *the only reason Jesus gives for not weeding out the tares (evil) is the harm it would do to the wheat (good).* We are simply not able to always accurately discern the good from the bad. There is a danger here of premature judgment. Jesus is telling us that judgment in these matters must be left to the end of the day and committed to the hands of God.

Do you know this hymn?

> There is a fountain filled with blood,
>   Drawn from Emmanuel's veins,
> And sinners plunged beneath that flood
>   Lose all their guilty stains.

Or this one—"O for a Closer Walk with God"?

> Where is the blessedness I knew
>   When first I saw the Lord?

Where is the soul-refreshing view
  Of Jesus and His word?
What peaceful hours I then enjoyed!
  How sweet their mem'ry still!
But they have left an aching void
  The world can never fill.

Return, O Holy Dove, return,
  Sweet messenger of rest;
I hate the sins that made Thee mourn
  And drove Thee from my breast.

William Cowper, a British poet who in the eighteenth century became the great hymnwriter for the evangelical movement in England, wrote those hymns. He also wrote the famous hymn "God Moves in Mysterious Ways, His Wonders to Perform."

He wrote that hymn on the eve of his second suicide attempt.[2]

Modern psychiatrists have diagnosed Cowper as "bipolar depressive." Throughout his lifetime, before and after his conversion, the poet moved in and out of severe bouts with depression, which he called "madness."

He lived the last quarter of his life in seclusion, never entering a church. But as one writer says, "His hymns were there. They are still there, giving a tongue to the pain of the doubter, the weak, and the sufferer. Every time I hear them now, I admire the man who kept on writing."[3]

Good and bad running on parallel tracks.

AND THEN THERE WAS . . .

George Matheson. Do you know his story? He was a bright young man with a promising future, engaged to be married. And then he began to lose his sight. Not wanting to be shackled to a blind man for the rest of her life, his fiancée broke off the engagement. Out of that heartbreak, Matheson wrote:

> O love, that wilt not let me go,
> I rest my weary soul in Thee.
> I give Thee back the life I owe,
> That in thine ocean depths its flow
> May richer, fuller be.

But my favorite verse is this one:

> O joy that seekest me through pain,
> I dare not shut my heart to Thee.
> I'll trace the rainbow through the rain,
> And feel the promise is not vain
> That morn shall tearless be.

O joy that seekest me through *pain!* I'll trace the rainbow through the *rain!* Good and bad running on parallel tracks. It is true that "our own best words and deeds must always be teased from our hearts' tangled motives."[4]

I met a couple in a Midwest city a few years ago whose story, though familiar, was no less painful. Their daughter fell in love with a boy they didn't approve of; he had, they felt, some serious character flaws. And they did what parents are wont to do with their daughters—they apprised her of their assessment of him and counseled her to break it off. And she did what daughters are wont to do—she ignored their advice (advice which actually spurred her onward) and married the boy. Unfortunately the parents were correct in their estimate of the young man; he did have some serious character flaws—and a few years and two babies later he abandoned her.

They could not tell their story without weeping. I hurt with them as they spoke of the pain and embarrassment and hardships through which their daughter had passed.

As I drove away that night I fantasized about being God. Do you ever do that? Do you ever say, "If I were God . . ."? Remember the old radio show "Queen for a Day"? I've always wanted to be God for a day. Boy, would I set some things right. It seems to me that God is letting power go to waste.

Anyway, I got to thinking how wonderful it would be if God granted me the power to turn back the calendar in the lives of that family. I would say to them, "Listen, God has given me the power to change everything that happened. I can turn back the clock and make it so your daughter will never meet that boy, never fall in love with him, never marry him, never be abandoned. I can make it where you will never know that heartache, never shed those tears. I can reverse this whole thing, and it will be as though it never happened. I can do that. Do you want me to? Just say the word and it will be done.

"Oh, there is one thing I should probably mention. You do realize that if I erase this terrible experience, you will have to give up those two grandbabies?

"You look startled. Well, you can't have it both ways, you know. If she never meets that boy, you'll never have those grandchildren.

"You say you don't want the pain? Well, I can get rid of that. What's that? You don't want to give up the children? Well, like I said. You can't have it both ways. You need to make up your mind. Which will it be?"

Now, I'm not a grandfather, so I can't speak with authority. But many a grandpa and grandma have told me they wouldn't give up their grandchildren, no matter what the pain.

How can we say that what happened in that family was totally evil when out of it came two precious lives you would die for? Good and bad run on parallel tracks, and they usually arrive about the same time.

THE MORNING AFTER

As the sun gently nudges its way into the eastern sky, Jacob's wives, Rachel and Leah, gather with their children and servants at the edge of the Jabbok stream.

The long night of waiting is over. Suddenly someone shouts, "There he is!"

Sure enough, it's Jacob crossing the stream. But wait—something's not right. He's limping.

"It looks like a bad limp," someone says. "Do you suppose he stumbled in the dark and twisted his leg?"

But as Jacob draws closer it's obvious more is wrong than just his limp. His clothes are dirty and torn; his face is bruised, his hair disheveled. Jacob looks as though he's been in a dogfight—and the dog won.

They rush to him. "Jacob, Jacob! What happened?"

"Oh," Jacob says, smiling, his eyes bright. "I got blessed last night."

Shaking their heads, they watch him as he limps away. Someone whispers: "Doesn't look like any victorious Christian I've ever seen."

BOOK
TWO
NAMING THE
SILENCES

Part One: Living Without Answers—
The Ministry of Silence

A dim aurora rises in the east,
Beyond the line of jagged questions hoar,
As if the head of our intombed High Priest
Began to glow behind the door:
Sure the gold wings will soon rise from the gray!
They rise not. Up I rise, press on the more,
To meet the slow coming of the Master's day.

George MacDonald

Distressed mind,
Forbear to tease the hooded why.
For the shape will not reply.

Edna St. Vincent Millay

When I lay these questions before God I get no answer. But
rather a special sort of "No answer." It is not the locked
door. It is more like a silent, certainly not uncompassion-
ate, gaze. As though He shook His head not in refusal but
waiving the question. Like, "Peace, child; you don't understand."

C. S. Lewis

CHAPTER

8

WHY?

My introduction to terror came five days after Christmas 1984.

We were visiting my mother-in-law and because she had six other houseguests, we were staying at a nearby motel. On our last evening we returned to the motel around midnight. I dropped my wife, daughter, and daughter-in-law (our son had returned earlier) at the lobby and drove around to the brightly lit parking lot at the rear of the motel. Finally finding a slot, I parked the car and grabbed a couple of small bags from the trunk. As I closed the trunk, a car with two men in the front seat pulled up behind. The man on the passenger side got out and came toward me, preceded by the stench of whiskey. When he spoke I could hardly understand him, but I knew he was asking directions to a certain street in the city. That's when I first suspected I was in trouble. You don't ask motel guests *local* street information. Besides, I now realized that I had seen this car cruising around the motel as I searched for a parking place.

"I don't know," I said and headed for the back door of the motel.

53

He came up behind me and grabbed my arm. "Gimme those bags!"

I jerked loose and hurried toward the door. He grabbed my arm again, spinning me around, and I found myself staring at a revolver in his left hand, pointing at my head.

"Gimme the bags!" he said.

His partner, still sitting behind the steering wheel, was yelling something I couldn't make out at first. Then I understood. He was yelling, "Kill him! Kill him!"

The man with the gun reached for my bags. "I'm gonna shoot you," he said.

I backed away, shaking my head, trying to decide if this was really happening and if this guy meant what he said. These things never happened this fast on TV.

While I was trying to convince myself this fellow wasn't serious, he shoved me back against a parked car. I tripped and landed flat on my back, still clinging to the two bags. The muzzle flashed with a loud pop, and I felt the bullet strike the pavement just to the right of my head. I remember thinking stupidly, "It's a .22."

If this clod was trying to kill me, I had nothing to lose by fighting back. I let go of the bags and grabbed for the gun. For a second I thought I had it. But even with his booze-soaked brain, he was stronger and enjoyed a decidedly superior position—me on my back and him straddling me. He cursed, jerked the gun away, and shook with anger. He shouted, "I'm gonna kill you, you—" and all I could think of was, "Dear God, I'm going to die in a Holiday Inn parking lot." No eloquent spiritual thoughts, no flashing revelations ("I saw heaven open and Saint Peter waving me up, an angelic chorus in the background belting out 'I'll Fly Away.'") My life didn't even pass before my eyes.

The gunman towered over me, pointing the gun at the space between my eyes. "I'm going to kill you," he said again.

In some primeval jerk of survival, I crossed my arms in front of my face, squeezed my eyes shut, and waited.

Nothing happened. I opened my eyes and saw him lower the gun, scoop up the bags, and run back to his car. Just as I was getting to my feet, I heard his partner say, "Go back and kill the—!" I was developing a real negative attitude toward that man.

The gunman muttered something, pitched my bags in his car, and headed my way. I knew I would never make it to the door of the motel—all I could do was dive behind a car and shrink into the smallest target possible.

He came about halfway to where I was, halted, wheeled around, and ran back to the car. I heard the car door slam and the tires squeal as the car sped away. Someone in the motel, hearing the gunshot, had come to a window and was watching and banging on the window. I suppose the gunman didn't want a witness. That witness probably saved my life.

At the trial six months later, the prosecuting attorney told the jury, "Mr. Dunn would not be here today if the defendant had been a better shot."

I agreed.

Later I remarked to a friend, "Thank God the fellow was a lousy shot."

"He wasn't a lousy shot," my friend said. "That had nothing to do with it. God was protecting you."

I agreed.

Another friend said, "Your guardian angel must have been sitting on your shoulder and knocked the bullet away."

I agreed.

But I remember a friend and his wife who were shot to death in their home a few years ago by intruders, and a disquieting question bullies its way into my mind, scattering my smug explanations: Where were their guardian angels the night they were murdered? Why didn't God protect them?

COMES AGAIN THE OLD QUESTION

When the hoped-for, prayed-for miracle doesn't come, when we are not delivered, when there is no miracle—this is the question that hounds us, making sleepless nights endless: Why?

Albert Camus spoke for many when he said, "I want everything to be explained to me or nothing. And the reason is impotent when it hears this cry from the heart. The mind aroused by this insistence seeks and finds nothing but contradictions and nonsense. . . . *If one could only say just once: 'This is clear,' then all would be saved.*"[1]

Let's face it: Life isn't fair. Injustice inhabits our world. Daily we are confronted with the elemental powers and fundamental forces of human existence, "the dark enigmas of life." We cannot escape the question of why it is so. "This little word 'why' is no torrent of speech. It is only a little drop of three letters. Yet it can cause mortal injury to our souls."[2] The question is pitiful, unavoidable—and normal.

I'm not fishing in a new pond. Sufferers of every age have struggled with this dark enemy. In Psalm 37, the writer speaks of fretting because of evildoers, of being envious against the workers of iniquity, of fretting because of the wicked man who prospers in his way and brings wicked devices to pass. In the 73rd Psalm, the psalmist airs his frustration, saying, "For I envied the arrogant when I saw the prosperity of the wicked."

I have conducted the funerals of fine, young Christian fathers and mothers, snatched away, suddenly and cruelly, and wondered at the rightness of a world where so many others, wicked and uncaring, stroll unscathed through the earth.

Columnist Jory Graham felt this same anger when stricken by cancer:

> Why me, and not that bum down the block who beats his wife and terrifies his kids? Why me, and not that power-drunk vice president who heads my department? Why me, just on the edge of achievement, rather than the crazed old woman who fishes about in garbage cans along the alley for the discards of our meals? Why me, and not the really evil people in our world?[3]

THE ATHEISTS HAVE A PRETTY GOOD ARGUMENT

C. S. Lewis, an atheist before his conversion, said that had anyone asked him during that time why he did not believe in God, he would have pointed to the injustices of the world. His answer, in part, would have been

> all stories will come to nothing: all life will turn out in the end to have been a transitory and senseless contortion upon the idiotic face of infinite matter. If you ask me to believe that this is the work of a benevolent and omnipotent spirit, I reply that all evidence points in the opposite direction. Either there is no spirit behind the universe, or else a spirit of indifference to good and evil, or else an evil spirit.[4]

Actually, the atheist has a good argument. "Why?" has always been an uncomfortable question because there is really no answer. It is the mischievous child who is a constant embarrassment to the rest of the family.

It isn't the everyday problems that turn our paradise into Pearl Harbor—it's the sneak attacks. We simply aren't prepared for the sharp curves life throws at us, those unannounced turns in the road. Just when we get a grip on life, our hands go numb and our exclamation points turn into question marks. The unexpected and the unexplained: This is what throws us off balance.

In the next two chapters, I'm going to try to regain my balance. I hope you'll follow me.

CHAPTER
9

WHY ME?

Christmas 1972, I gave my wife a gold watch. On the back was inscribed:

> To Kaye, with love
> 1972
> "A Very Good Year"

I didn't know it was the last good year we would have for quite a while.

Early in 1973 our fifteen-year-old son, Ronnie, Jr. seemed suddenly, as it appeared to us then, to change personalities, as though he had become a different person. His school work began to suffer; he became moody, one day feeling on top of the world, the next day angry, withdrawn, irritable, hostile—the next day loathing himself for having acted so badly.

We had no idea what had happened, was happening, to our son. At first, I assumed it was a spiritual problem. For the next three years, in spite of our prayers and best efforts, the situation worsened.

After a suicide attempt we admitted him to the psychiatric ward of a hospital for two weeks of tests. He was diagnosed manic depressive, a mood disorder caused by a chemical imbalance in the blood, which recurrently plunged him into deep depression. His illness was bipolar, which meant that he alternated between elation and despair.

The doctor put him on a new miracle drug, Lithium, plus Stelazine and Elavil. He improved immediately. One of my most vivid and happiest (?) memories was when Ronnie found out that it wasn't his fault, that an illness was making him act that way.

Encouraged by knowing what was wrong and that medicine and treatment were available, Kaye and I prayed with great confidence. We had no doubt God would deliver our son; we had a number of promises we believed God had given us. I *knew* that one day he would enter the ministry and live a fruitful life serving God. Our nightmare was over. That was August 1975.

Three months later, on Thanksgiving Day, Ronnie, Jr. took his life.

The doctor had warned us that patients like Ronnie, Jr. often began feeling so good, they would skip a dose of the medicine or forget to take it. But the balance of the chemicals and medicine in his blood was so delicate, missing even one dose could spell disaster. Each morning Kaye would lay out his daily dosage for him to take with him to school (he was not allowed to take an entire bottle of medicine to school). On a couple of occasions as Kaye did the laundry she found his medicine still in his shirt pocket.

On a cold, gray December afternoon a few friends and relatives gathered with us around a gray casket bearing the remains of eighteen years of laughter and tears, tricycles and baseball bats, pain and hope, short pants and driving lessons. When the casket was lowered into the earth I buried with it a lifetime of easy answers and un-asked questions—except one: *Why?* I'm still trying to bury that one.

Besides the normal anguish of such a loss, the survivors of this kind of tragedy have a double burden: Not only must they struggle with the grief, but they must also contend with the singular guilt and stigma that attach themselves to suicide.

Writing of her son's suicide, psychiatrist Sue Chance says, "All I could think was, 'If you want to *really* be a failure in life, have your child commit suicide.' It's bad enough to lose a child and my heart really does go out to other bereaved parents, but the guilt you have over not getting them to the doctor 'soon enough,' the guilt over not being able to protect them from cancer or drunk drivers or whatever can't be as fundamental and soulsearing as knowing they couldn't endure the life you gave them."[1]

And then there are the insensitive people like the fellow who asked me, "Do you believe suicides go to hell?"

But there was something else that made Ronnie, Jr.'s death more painful. Several close friends were also having serious trouble with their teenagers; some had even been arrested on drug charges. Bound by a mutual burden, our families had formed a unique fraternity, praying for one another, all believing God would honor our faith and answer our prayers.

Ronnie was the only one who didn't make it. While God restored the others, it appeared He had ignored our prayers. I confess I found it difficult to rejoice with the other parents when their prodigals returned. Once I refused to take a phone call from a friend who was calling to tell me of his son's homecoming and salvation. I didn't want to hear good news about somebody else's son.

At first, of course, I tried to be "spiritual" and "victorious." I refused to question God. I gave "thanks in everything," voiced my "Praise the Lords" like a good Catholic doing his "Hail Marys" or a heathen spinning his prayer wheel. But the days became weeks and the weeks months, and I knew Ronnie was never coming back home. I felt cheated and betrayed. As the anesthesia of shock wore off, the reality of his death settled on me like a black fog until finally the suppressed anger and hurt erupted with "*Why, God?*" which was more of an accusation than a question. It really is an accusation, you know. The Hebrew word for "why," used most frequently in the Psalms, is "both a cry of lament and protest. It places the issue of human suffering before and in front of God. It is to ask why, for what reason, to what end, does [He] remain silent. It also assumes that this suffering is unjust."[2]

But for all my crying and pleading and threatening, all I got was a silence that was absolute and awesome—a silence in heaven.

Because I believe grief is a private occupation, I am reluctant to write about it. I am not parading my woe in search of sympathy. My story merits no special telling; little about it is unique. Many others have fought the same—and worse—losing battle. Then why am I telling my story? I do it for myself as much as for you.

WHY DO WE KEEP ASKING WHY?

William Miller is right on target when he says:

Because the need for answers appears so strongly, if we cannot come up with some actual answer, reason or explanation, we will create or manufacture one of our own. It may not make much sense to objective viewers, but it will satisfy the need. In fact a lot of the "answers" people come up with through rationalizations are nothing more than euphemisms and platitudes. Nevertheless, they do meet the need to explain and thus make acceptance of loss more bearable.[3]

Ours is "the public's right to know" generation. We demand an explanation for everything, and a vigilant and accommodating news media keeps us informed on everything from Jimmy Carter's hemorrhoids to Ronald Reagan's colon to George Bush's malice toward broccoli to Bill Clinton's haircuts. These days Congress does more investigating than legislating (which may be a blessing). Privacy has become a fossil of an earlier age.

But while journalists, lawmakers, and fortunetellers operate by that policy, God does not. He operates strictly on "a need to know" basis.

But still we ask: What is so magical, so healing about knowing why? Let me suggest some reasons.

For one thing, an unanswered "why" disturbs the *orderliness of life* we believe in. We like to think we live in an ordered universe where everything makes sense. For everything that happens there is a logical explanation; every effect has some discernible cause.

It has always been this way. James Crenshaw writes: "In order to render life bearable the ancients posited a belief in order, both in the macrocosm and the microcosm. The universe was predictable, within limits, for it was subject to the wishes of the Creator. . . . So long as that conviction of order held firm in the universe, essential meaning remained intact despite occasional disturbances that made happiness an elusive goal."[4]

Anthropologists tell us that from the beginning human-kind has believed that we could control life. The rituals of preliterate man were based on the belief that the power or spirit of an animal could be transferred to the worshiper by sacrificing the creature, or that the strength of an enemy could be transferred by taking his scalp. At first man sought to control life with rituals and altars. Ernest Becker writes: "By means of the techniques of ritual men imagined that they took firm control of the material world, and at the same time transcended that world by fashioning their own invisible projects which made them supernatural, raised them over and above material decay and death."[5]

As civilization advanced, the rituals and altars gave way to science and machines. These were enthroned as the new talismans. We deified machines and placed our trust in them. Eventually we made the unhappy discovery that machines are fallible; they break down, and with them our security.

In an effort to recapture the control of life, we returned to the rituals and the altars (not necessarily to Christian rituals and altars), some to prayer and faith. For many, prayer and faith are not the means of doing God's will; they are the rituals and altars whereby we *control our lives.* Effective use of them, so we think, enables us to rise above the afflictions and accidents of human existence. And often our use of them is just as magical as the rituals of primitive man.

The point is, we demand an ordered and controlled world. Everything that happens must have a logical explanation. If our car won't start, it's out of gas or the battery is dead. If the house lights go out, there's a power failure somewhere along the line or we didn't pay last month's bill. If we are not healed, a religious witchdoctor divines the cause as sin or lack of faith.

We must have a logical explanation—all neat and tidy, every board nailed down. Life is not a cosmic throw of the dice, not a giant, outrageous crap shoot. Our existence or extinction does not hang by the thread of some fickle fate. This kind of world view creates security and maintains sanity. But an unanswered "why?" jeopardizes all that.

Helmut Thielicke puts it this way:

> For long stretches . . . we go on living our lives fairly innocuously, with no particular problems. Life simply pursues its course. We observe that evil does not pay, that success comes to the diligent, and that idlers finally come to grief.
>
> But suddenly something happens that sounds like a broken axle in this smoothly rotating machine of life. We are confronted with a contradiction which we simply cannot explain. . . .
>
> Are we not surrounded on every side with these dark enigmas, which are so hard to shake off, once they are discovered? Why is it that just when life reaches its supreme moments we should suddenly be overtaken by the dread mortality and the fragility of life?[6]

Another reason: If a logical explanation can be found, we can *prevent a repetition of the tragedy.* It need not happen again—especially to us. Later we will examine the healing of the blind man in John's Gospel. The disciples, you remember, asked Jesus whose sin had caused the man's affliction, his own or his parents. I've often wondered what motivated their question. Was it more than theological curiosity? Perhaps lurking in the back of their minds was the idea that if they could discover the specific sin that caused his blindness, they could avoid it. Whatever else happened to them, they wouldn't go blind.

Could it be that our own urgency to know why arises from the fear that the same thing could happen to us? I have a feeling that often when we pray for another's healing, we are really praying for our own. It's like sending a scout ahead of the main party to see if the natives are friendly. We're testing the waters. If God heals this one, it is possible He will do the same for us. It sustains a desperate hope that we can postpone the inevitable. Our own life is riding on that prayer.

Perhaps this was what those friends of Job thought. Warren Wiersbe tells us that Job's plight was a threat to his friends. "His experience challenged the validity of their cut-and-dried theology. . . . This meant that what happened to Job *could happen to them!* They were not really interested in Job as a hurting person. Their major concern was in Job as a problem to be removed, not as a person to be encouraged."[7]

People like Job are an embarrassment. Their unrelieved suffering throws a wrench into our theological machine and forces us to invent excuses for failure and exceptions to the rule. And we are an inventive bunch.

Then, we may ask why because *we seek absolution* from guilt. Guilt is the inevitable consequence of grief. And nothing is as irrational as guilt born of grief. Somehow in the sorrow-soaked thought process we see ourselves as partly or wholly to blame for whatever happened. We either caused it, contributed to it, or failed to prevent it. Guilt charges us with not loving enough, not doing enough, not—being enough. Surely, somehow we could have averted the danger, and that eats at us.

But an explanation that proves we didn't cause it, or could not have prevented it ("it was God's will"), absolves us of guilt. Especially is this true with survivors of suicide—we want it to be an accident or foul play—anything but suicide. Suicide accuses.

So great is the need for absolution we may in the presence of others accuse ourselves openly because we want them to come to our defense and affirm our innocence.

Further, in asking why we seek *moral equalization.* The question "Why me?" assumes an injustice has been done, one that demands redress. "The 'why me?' focuses only on the arbitrariness and unfairness of the situation. It imprisons one within the chaos."[8]

We hardly ever ask, "Why *not* me?" Later, perhaps, but not at first. Whatever has happened, we certainly didn't deserve it; we are innocent bystanders struck by a stray bullet. We never question the good things, only the bad. Dr. M. Scott Peck makes this observation: "It's a strange thing. Dozens of times I have been asked by patients or acquaintances: 'Dr. Peck, why is there evil in the world?' Yet no one has asked me in all these years, 'Why is there good in the world?'"[9]

Not long ago a young man in our city was killed in a car wreck. Neither he nor any of his family were Christians. The mortuary asked one of the ministers at our church to conduct the funeral service. The day before the funeral he went to the family's home to discuss the service. As he prepared to leave he asked the young man's mother if he could have a word of prayer with them. The mother became enraged and shouted at the minister, "There will be no praying in this house! God took my son from me! No, no praying in this house!"

When the minister related the incident, I thought: That's probably the first time she's given God any thought in years. And probably the first time she's given Him credit for doing anything. I doubt that when her son was born she gave any thought to God or acknowledged His part in the birth—only in the death.

Why is it we blame God only for the bad things that happen to us? Why do insurance companies describe natural disasters and catastrophes as "acts of God"? We never question the positive points of life, only the bad. We are not amazed at God's goodness; we take it for granted, as though it is owed to us. Badness surprises us; goodness does not.

Although discovering the why will not really change anything, it will restore the sense of fairness we believe (or desperately want to believe) is built into God's creation. After all, if it is God's world, it must be founded on justice and equality. That just makes sense. "In short," writes James Crenshaw, "the one who brought the world into being possesses sufficient power to insure a balance of order and equity. That is why again and again sages brought together the concept of creation and justice."[10]

Consider also that the question may be an attempt to *vindicate God.* "Why?" is really "Why, God?" The question is, in fact, addressed to a God who is absolutely sovereign, and as my theology professor used to say, "The sovereignty of God means that God can do as He pleases—and that quite well." To believe in an all-powerful, all-caring God is to believe that He is somehow involved in everything that happens, and when something evil happens it tarnishes His image.

Theologians have a name for this: theodicy, which may loosely be defined as "the attempt to pronounce a verdict of 'not guilty' over God for whatever seems to destroy the order of society and the universe."[11]

If God is sovereign, we are obligated to say that God either directly caused it to happen or allowed it to happen—either way He could have prevented it. And to the one suffering, the difference between the two is of profound indifference. We say with Abraham, "Shall not the Judge of all the earth do right?" (Gen. 18:25). Or with Gideon we ask, "If the LORD is with us, why then has all this happened to us?" (Judg. 6:3).

In his book *When the Gods Are Silent*, Kornelis Miskotte, speaking of the horrors of Auschwitz, asks a chilling question: "One can still 'believe' in the God who permitted to happen what did happen, but can one still speak to Him?"[12]

In the aftermath of tragedy, to gather up the debris of our faith, we call God on the carpet and demand He explain Himself, and He had better have a good reason for doing what He did. But the truth is that God, being God, doesn't need to explain His actions to anyone.

Finally, and perhaps fundamentally, we ask why because *we cannot live with mystery*. This computerized, televised age has declared mystery unacceptable; anything, everything must be disassembled, X-rayed, photographed, identified, and classified. When we ask why, what we are after is a simple, pat explanation of what has happened, thus evading the drudgery of thinking and the inconvenience of mystery.

The explosive popularity of the Health-and-Wealth movement is not surprising. It promises simple answers to every question and easy solutions to every difficulty. We are relieved of the task of (God forbid!) thinking for ourselves. Everything has been done for us. People want answers, guarantees; they want a leader, brimming with confidence, who says, "Yes, I know, and I will tell you." The will and power of God have been captured like a butterfly in the nets of those "who know what it's all about," and recast in a money-back guaranteed formula: "Push, pull, click, click—get an answer that quick."

Still the mystery stands. But as Gabriel Marcel points out, "A strange thing; suffering is, in fact, only capable of taking on . . . spiritual meaning in so far as it implies an unfathomable mystery."[13]

But one day while I was struggling to unmask this question, a thought struck me: What if I'm asking the wrong question?

CHAPTER
10

WHAT NOW?

The thought struck a second time: There is no answer to the question "Why?" because that is not a legitimate question. We can't expect to find the right answer if we are asking the wrong question—and I believe we are.

For months I had been compiling from the Bible and other sources answers to the question—about a dozen. They were, I believe, all correct—as far as they went. But even with a dozen answers the question remained unanswered. Or perhaps it is more accurate to say that the answers were unsatisfying. The ache was still there.

I talked recently to a father whose son died tragically. As he recounted the boy's death and its aftermath, he said he could see good things that had come out of it; several relatives had turned to Christ.

"But it's not enough," he said suddenly. "It's not enough."

Who is qualified to argue with him? I suspect the only thing that would satisfy the mother whose little girl has been raped and murdered would be to have her daughter back, alive and well. We may argue (and rightly so) that the death of a child will work to the glory of God. But grieving parents may be forgiven for crying, "Let God get His glory somewhere else; give us back our child." I hope so, for I have spoken similar words.

A few years ago a jumbo jet crashed a couple of miles from our house, killing over 130 people. Miraculously, about 30 passengers survived. One was a young man whose wife and two children died in the crash. A woman tried to console him by saying, "You're still young. You can remarry and have more children."

I knew a family of nine children. One died. A would-be comforter said, "You still have eight wonderful children."

But that means nothing. *Eighty* more children could not replace the one you lost. Such consolation comes off sounding as though people do not take our tragedy seriously. One person's answer is another's enigma. One person's explanation is another's despair.

Don't misunderstand. I believe that when we stand on the credit side of eternity and know as well as we are known, we will agree with everything God did—"Yes, it was best to do it that way. I see that now." We will be satisfied and lodge no complaints. Meanwhile an answer in the hand is worth a dozen in heaven.

Therefore "Why?" is the wrong question, for in the end it solves nothing. When others out of a sincere desire to comfort try to force their answers upon us, we may reply in the words of an earlier sufferer: "How then will you comfort me with empty nothings? There is nothing left of your answers but falsehood" (Job 21:34, NRSV).

C. S. Lewis describes the outcome of his own search for an answer:

Meanwhile, where is God? This is one of the most disquieting symptoms. When you are happy, so happy you have no sense of needing Him, if you turn to Him with praise, you will be welcomed with open arms. But go to Him when your need is desperate, when all other help is vain and what do you find? A door slammed in your face, and a sound of bolting and double bolting on the inside. After that, silence. You may as well turn away.[1]

Our failure is not that we do not find the right answers; it is that we do not ask the right questions. As Christopher Morely said, "I had a million questions to ask God: but when I met Him, they all fled my mind; and it didn't matter."[2]

As our knowledge of and fellowship with God deepen, the more we will trust Him, and the more we trust Him, the less our need to understand. Once we recognize this, peace of mind lies within our reach.

SOME BIBLICAL LIGHT

The ninth chapter of John's Gospel tells the story of a man born blind and his encounter with Christ. This particular blind man caught the eye of Jesus. In those days the roads were littered with pitiful individuals who, because of some handicap, were forced to play the role of a beggar. The sight was so common that people viewed them, not as persons of worth, but as a bothersome species to be tolerated (they had what we would call "compassion burnout").

But when the Bible says that Jesus "saw" this blind man, it uses a word that means "to look with rapt attention." It was not a casual glance, unregistered by the brain. In fact, Jesus gave him such a fixed stare that the disciples noticed it, and they, too, became interested in the man's case—but only as a theological curiosity.

Their question reflected the conventional religious mentality of the day: "Rabbi, who sinned, this man or his parents, that he was born blind?" (John 9:2). Notice they did not ask, "*Did* someone sin?" but "*Who* sinned?"

There was no question in their minds that sin had caused the blindness; the only question was *whose* sin. And they were not referring to sin in general, which is common to all; no, they had in mind a specific sin, the judgment of said sin being the poor man's blindness.

According to the prevailing theology of that day, sin always brought suffering, therefore, if one was suffering some physical malady, it was a foregone conclusion that he had brought it upon himself by specific sin, or by the sin of his parents. Unjust suffering was inconceivable to the disciples—as it is to us. Suffering implies guilt.

So entrenched in their minds was this belief that they were happily oblivious to the inanity of their question. One might understand if it were the parents' sin that caused the affliction, but if the man was *born* blind, how in heaven's name could *his* sin be the culprit? An ancient pagan belief, not generally shared by the Jews, held that a man *could sin* in his pre-existent state. Others believed that some were punished in anticipation of the sins they would commit during their lifetime. In other words, pay now, sin later. But again, this was a pagan doctrine, not a Jewish one. Still, the disciples were so certain that all infirmities were the consequences of specific sin that they asked this stupid question. With their faulty theology they painted themselves into a corner.

And so they too looked upon this man. But not with compassion; he was merely a theological conversation piece, a specimen to be examined under the microscope of curiosity.

Jesus' answer must have stunned them: "It was neither that this man sinned, nor his parents; but it was in order that the works of God might be displayed in him" (John 9:3 NAS). He did not mean, of course, that neither the man nor his parents had *never* sinned, for all have sinned. Rather, He was saying that it was not a particular sin that had brought divine judgment in the form of blindness. The man was not suffering because of sin.

So much for the pat theology of the disciples. They were interested in the *cause* of the man's blindness; they wanted to dive into the man's past and dredge up some sordid but satisfying explanation. They offered Jesus two possible reasons, and He rejected them both.

What is surprising, having rejected their two suggestions, is that Jesus did not offer a *third* possibility. He shed no light on this mystery, neither here nor elsewhere. Rather, He opened up an entirely new view of the matter. To Jesus, the man's blindness was neither divine chastisement nor simple chance. It was a challenge. Jesus appears totally disinterested in the why of the case. For the backward view of the disciples, He offers His own forward look. The real question was not "Why was this man born blind?" but "What are we going to do about it?" He was more interested in consequences than causes.

Let's look carefully at the answer He gave to the disciples: But it was in order "that the works of God might be displayed in him" (John 9:3 NAS).

At first glance it appears that God deliberately blinded the man just to provide an opportunity to display His works. But that is a wrong conclusion. While the little Greek word translated "that" *(hina)* normally indicates "in order that," a phrase expressing purpose, this is one of the few instances where it is not used in that manner. Here the construction of the Greek New Testament makes it refer, not to *purpose*, but to *result*. "*Hina* (that) here seems to express result, an unusual, but not unparalleled use."[3] Turner and Mantey in their work on the Gospel of John agree that "*hina* introduces a result, not a purpose clause here."[4]

In other words, God is not charged with causing the man's condition; rather, the man may be rescued by the glorifying works of God, works that manifest His mercy and power. This is the most critical point of the story: What is needed here is not answers, but action.

"The man is not to be treated as an instrument merely but a living representative of the mercy of God. His suffering is the occasion and not the appointed preparation for the miracle, though when we regard things from the divine side we are constrained to see them in their dependence on the will of God."[5]

And so the question remains unanswered because the real issue is not where it came from, but what we are going to do with it. More important than discovering the origin of suffering is the display of God's works in the midst of that suffering. Philip Yancey correctly observes, "The emphasis I see in the Bible is not to look backward and find out if God is responsible in order to accuse Him. . . . The emphasis is rather on looking ahead to what God can make of seeming tragedy."[6]

By His answer Jesus was in effect saying, "This man was born blind and that is a fact. Dwelling on 'Why?' is not going to solve anything. Now that it has happened, let God's glory be seen."[7]

As I write, it suddenly occurs to me that Lazarus was never interviewed! His testimony of what it means to be brought back from the dead, what it's like to be dead, what he saw when he was dead—none of these things is mentioned.

Had He wanted to, Jesus could have answered every question and solved every mystery of human existence. Why didn't He tell us how to invent the telephone, build an airplane, discover a cure for cancer? Jesus could have laid bare every secret of life, of death, and of eternity. Why didn't He? He could have saved everybody a lot of trouble if He had. It's incredible to realize that Jesus ignored the issues that occupy our minds and twist our hearts. That was not His concern, and He is telling His disciples it should not be theirs. This thought is reinforced in the Gospel of Luke:

"Now on the same occasion there were some present who reported to Him about the Galileans, whose blood Pilate had mingled with their sacrifices.

"And He answered and said to them, 'Do you suppose that these Galileans were greater sinners than all other Galileans, because they suffered this fate?

"'I tell you, no, but, unless you repent, you will all likewise perish.'

"'Or do you suppose that those eighteen on whom the tower in Siloam felled and killed them, were worse culprits than all the men who live in Jerusalem?

"'I tell you, no, but, unless you repent, you will all likewise perish.'" (Luke 13:1–5 NAS)

With these words, Jesus lifts the burden of guilt from every hurting heart. He makes it clear that those slaughtered by wicked rulers like Pilate or those killed in a freak accident such as happened at Siloam are not objects of divine retribution.

And having ruled out divine judgment as the cause of those two disasters, Jesus still does not explain "why" they happened. Refusing to be drawn into extraneous debate, He pins them to the mat with the searing declaration, "Unless *you* repent, you will all likewise perish!" I am not here, Jesus is saying, to answer the riddles of life; I am here to do My Father's will. Instead of nosing about in the inscrutables of human existence, you would do better to see to your own souls.

Jesus refused to answer the why of suffering because that is not the ultimate issue. The ultimate issue is how we are to respond to that suffering and the message it delivers. Hans Küng writes:

> . . . Jesus was aware of all the suffering, all the pain, all the grief. But in the face of all the evil, Jesus did not give any philosophical or theological justification, any theodicy. . . . This is not a God at an ominous, transcendent distance, but close in incomprehensible goodness; he is a God who does not make empty promises about the hereafter or minimize the present darkness, futility and meaninglessness. Instead, in darkness, futility and meaninglessness, he invites us to the venture of hope.[8]

FROM "WHY ME?" TO "WHAT NOW?"

"Why me?" is a useless question, for in the end it solves nothing. Only when we face up to the inadequacy of this question will we be free to ask the right one.

The *right* question, the one put forth by Christ Himself, is *"what now?"* This question transforms the landscape of suffering from a random, accidental absurdity to a vital part of the grand scheme of a great God.

The "why me?" stance afflicts us with tunnel vision, making it impossible to see anything but the "unfairness" of our predicament. "It imprisons one within the chaos. It destroys the ability to retain a meaningful existence. . . . It implies . . . the individual is not only not whole in body, but also fragmented in spirit."[9]

But "what now?" allows us to step outside that prison and see ourselves, not as hapless victims, but as objects of divine attention. Helmut Thielicke describes God as a "God of ends." Commenting on the response of Christ to the disciples' question, he says:

> No, it is not that He has nothing to say. He tells the people: your question is wrongly put. . . . Thus, by rejecting the question, Jesus helps to liberate us from the constant complaint against God and from the injury we do ourselves thereby. . . . For He teaches us to put our question in a way which is meaningful. He tells us that we should not ask, "Why?" but "To what end?"[10]

"What now?" breaks the trance of *self-pity*. We are self-centered and self-interested creatures. Our frame of reference is ourselves. Because we have created a new heaven and a new earth with ourselves as their center, this "egocentric structure" restricts our thinking to the orbit of our own little universe.

Egocentric people are miserable beings. Peace of mind eludes them because they are unable to achieve the one thing they need most: to determine their own destiny. They live on the ragged edge of panic because they know with fatal certainty that sooner or later life is going to get out of hand; they cannot forever deny that their fate lies outside their jurisdiction.

Self-pity absorbs us, devours us; it warps our thinking and distorts our vision—of ourselves, of others, and of God. Bitter, sour, and cynical—that's the kind of person self-pity creates.

Jory Graham's experience with the "why me?" of cancer is helpful:

If we are not to sink into chronic depression and helpless anger, we have to go beyond the futile attempt to find an answer to *why me?* to acceptance of the fact that we have cancer: *I have it. Now what do I do?* This is the decision that will give meaning and significance to the rest of our lives, despite physical limitations, recurrent frustration and fear.[11]

When we ask "What now?" we shift our focus from ourselves to God and what He is up to in our lives. And He is up to something. But we will never see it with our eyes turned selfward. If we can say to our adversities what Joseph said to his brothers—"And as for you, you meant evil against me, but God meant it for good" (Gen. 50:20 NAS)—we will gain a fresh, confident, and creative direction in life. God does not give an answer to every "why?" but He gives assurance to every "who."

Not only does "what now?" save us from self-pity, but it also gives us *something to look forward to.* "What now?" means we are still moving, still growing. In short, we have a *future.* It means that life can be good again. And this is essential, for there is nothing more bleak than a future that can never be better than the past; nothing more hopeless than believing the best is behind us, that no matter how good life may be, no matter how many good things come to us, life can never be as good as it once was.

Take my word for it, I've been there. Like ancient Israel, we want to hang our harps in the willows, for how can we sing the song of the Lord in a strange land?

Not long ago a middle-aged couple approached me after a service, introduced themselves, and said some nice things about the message. Then the woman said, "It was good to see you smile."

That was a new one. "Well," I said, "thank you."

"No, I really mean it," she said. "It was good to see you smile."

"Well," I said again, "thank you. I'm glad you liked it."

She took my hand and looked at me with a hint of tears in her eyes. "You don't know what I'm talking about, do you?"

"No, I really don't."

"Six months ago," she said, "Our daughter was killed in a car wreck. She was only seventeen. I've not been able to handle it, to accept it. I felt that life would never be worth living again, that I could never be happy again. When we heard you were speaking here tonight—we knew you'd had a similar experience—well, we thought maybe you could help us . . . me, somehow. I wanted to see how you were doing. And tonight as you were speaking, you were smiling, and suddenly I knew it was possible to be happy again, that someday I would be able to smile again. I thought I never would, but seeing you smile, I know I can too—someday."

I was reminded of the psalmist's words in Psalm 42. He is swamped with despair and depression. He has what Ray Stedman called "The King David Blues." But in the eleventh verse, he says, "Hope in God, for I shall *yet* praise Him" (my emphasis). There are times when we are unable to praise God; we try, but the words stick in our throat. We are so overwhelmed that we are unable to praise, or even pray, or even believe.

But we will not always drink the bitter cup. God will do for us what He did for Moses and the Israelites in Exodus 15. On their march from Egypt they came to a place called Marah. It was called Marah because the water there was bitter, and the people became bitter because of it, and griped to Moses. But Moses "cried out to the LORD, and the LORD showed him a tree; and he threw it into the waters, and the waters became sweet" (v. 25 NAS).

And then God led them to Elim "where there were twelve springs of waters [that's one for every tribe], and seventy date palms [that's one for every elder], and they camped there beside the waters" (v. 27 NAS).

By the way, Elim was only about five miles from Marah. Marah today; Elim tomorrow. Bitterness today; sweetness tomorrow.

Are you at Marah? We've all made our stops there, where life becomes so bitter we can't swallow it, when the things that once were sweet and refreshing, once a source of joy, become sour to the taste and depressing to the spirit. I believe that if we look to God and cry out to Him, He will open our eyes to see a tree, a something, invisible to faithless eyes and prayerless hearts, that will restore the sweetness to our lives. "What now?" expresses our belief that there is an Elim in our future.

It is God's style to save the best until last. In that great book of remembrance, Deuteronomy, Moses reminds the people that even in the worst of times, God's intention was to do good to them. "In the wilderness He fed you with manna which your fathers did not know, that He might humble you and that He might test you, *to do good for you in the end*" (Deut. 8:16 KJV, emphasis added).

He sent the same message through Jeremiah to the Babylonian captives: "For thus says the LORD, 'When seventy years have been completed for Babylon, I will visit you and fulfil My good word to you, to bring you back to this place. For I know the plans that I have for you,' declares the LORD, 'plans for welfare and not for calamity *to give you a future and a hope'"* (Jer. 29:10–11 NAS, emphasis added).

And, of course, there's Job. "And the LORD restored the fortunes of Job when he prayed for his friends, and the LORD increased all that Job had twofold. . . . And the LORD blessed *the latter days of Job more than his beginning*" (Job 42:10, 12 NAS, emphasis added).

When through the settling dust of collapsed hopes we can ask, "What now?" we are testifying to a faith that believes God saves the best until last.

Finally, asking "What now?" makes us *a part of God's work.* Look again at John 9:3, "Jesus answered, 'It was neither that this man sinned, nor his parents; but *it was* in order that the works of God might be displayed in him.'" Notice that I italicized the words *it was*—because they are italicized in the King James Version, which means they were added by the translators to make the verse read more smoothly. They are not a part of the original text. Nor is the period at the end of verse 3. Now let's read that part of the verse again, omitting the italicized words and the period, right on to verse 4:

> "But in order that the works of God might be displayed in him, we must work the work of Him who sent me, as long as it is day; the night is coming, when no man can work."

Jesus is not saying that the man was born blind just so the works of God could be displayed. He is saying that the man was born blind, *period.* No explanation, no discussion. Now, in order that the works of God may be displayed in him, let's get to work. Again, the issue is not "why?" but "what now?"

Take a closer look at the word *works.* Jesus is about to perform—a miracle? Yes, but He calls it work. What is to us a miracle is to Jesus simply work. It's all in a day's work. Everyday, ordinary work.

The word *miracle* does not appear in John's Gospel. He uses two words to describe "miracles"—*works* and *signs*. *Sign* occurs 17 times in John (11 times the King James translates it "miracles") and seems to be John's favorite. Why?

John is saying that miracles of healing themselves are not strategic, but what they *indicate*, what they point to or *signify*. Jesus did not perform miracles because He came to perform miracles. He came to reveal the Father, and a miracle was a peg on which He could hang a text.

You may think I am making much ado about nothing by insisting on the word *work* rather than *miracle*, but there is a reason. Our categories of thinking about God and miracles are all fouled up.

One night while waiting for a service to begin, I overheard two women seated behind me. They were talking about a car wreck in which one boy was killed and another injured. The injured boy was obviously the son of one of the women, for one woman said to the other, "I'm so glad you're son is all right."

"Yes," said the other woman, "God is good."

But I couldn't help wondering what the mother of the dead boy was saying about God. And I wondered if the son of the woman behind me had been killed, if she would still say, "God is good."

It occurs to me that God and the devil have something in common: They both get blamed for a lot of things they don't do. Why is it when something unpleasant comes along we immediately credit it to the devil? Sometimes Satan's greatest triumph is making us believe that the one chipping away at us is the devil instead of God. I refer you back to Jacob.

We must learn to see the supernatural in the natural. We must know that the rising of the sun is as much a work of

God as the raising of Lazarus. Both events are children of the same Father. And it may be that the very thing that makes us think God is not at work is the very work that God is working at. Elizabeth Barrett Browning wrote, "Earth is crammed with heaven, and every common bush afire with God, but only he who sees it removes his shoes. The rest sit around it and pluck blackberries."

A final observation: A whole man would have been of little use to Jesus that day. To display the works of God, He needed someone with an unanswered "why?" in his life.

As for myself, I confess I'm still trying to get an answer to my "why?" And I'm still getting the silent treatment. But it's all right. I trust Him.

For the present I'll settle for a "what now?"

Part Two: Will a Person Serve God for Nothing?—
The Ministry of Suffering

Tragedy is not denied: the tragic vision is affirmed, even as it is transcended.

W. Lee Humphreys

Through these months, *acceptance* has been a word of liberty and victory and peace to me. But it has never meant acquiescence in illness. . . . But it did mean contentment with the unexplained.

Amy Carmichael

I consider that our present sufferings are not worth comparing with the glory that will be revealed in us.

Paul, Romans 8:18 (NIV)

CHAPTER
11

THE WAGER

Once upon a time, in a faraway land, there lived a man, just and wise, humble and charitable. His riches and his virtues aroused jealousy in heaven and on earth. His name was Job.

Through the problems he embodied and the trials he endured, he seems familiar—even contemporary. We know his history for having lived in it. In times of stress it is to his words that we turn to express our anger, revolt or resignation. He belongs to our most intimate landscape, the most vulnerable part of our past.

Elie Wiesel, *Messengers of God*

One Saturday morning my phone rang, and when I answered it an angry voice blurted out: "Take my name off the church roll—I'm not coming back!"

The voice was familiar, but I couldn't place it. "Excuse me. What did you say?"

"I said take my name off the church roll. I'm not coming back!"

Then I recognized the voice, and I knew what had happened.

The man's son had been in trouble with the law several times but had recently committed a major crime and was in danger of doing hard time at the grown-up prison.

Just a few days before, I had accompanied the father to the courthouse where we met with the judge, the prosecuting attorney, the boy's juvenile case worker, and the boy's lawyer. It didn't look good for the young man. Considering his past record and this last offense, which included kidnapping, the authorities were disinclined to send the boy back to the juvenile lock-up.

Later, as we walked from the courthouse, the father said, "I know they won't send him to the state prison."

"Oh," I said. "You do?"

"Yes. I've prayed about it, and I know God won't let that happen to him."

And so when the father called that Saturday morning, vowing never to return to church, I knew what had happened. God had "let" the authorities send his son to state prison.

I never think about that churchmember without thinking of the question Satan put to God concerning a man named Job.

Do you know Job? He's the man in the Old Testament of whom God said, "There is no one on earth like him; he is blameless and upright, a man who fears God and shuns evil" (Job 1:8 NIV). That's quite a résumé, and it's said of him three times.[1] And remember, this is God speaking, not Job's publicist.

Job is presented to us in ideal terms, a model person who exemplifies the virtues that everybody ought to have, the kind of person we all long to be. Here is man at his best—Man of the Year.

How good is Job? He's so good that God bragged on him. To the devil. Let's listen to this strange conversation between God and Satan, the Adversary.

> One day the angels came to present themselves before the LORD, and Satan also came with them. The LORD said to Satan, "Where have you come from?"
>
> Satan answered the LORD, "From roaming through the earth and going back and forth in it."
>
> Then the LORD said to Satan, "Have you considered my servant Job? There is no one on earth like him; he is blameless and upright, a man who fears God and shuns evil." (Job 1:6–8)

Hold everything! It wasn't Satan who brought up Job's name—it was God. All Job's soon-to-arrive problems came because God bragged on him. That makes me want to ask the Lord to keep my name out of any future conversations He may have with the devil.

Anyway, Satan responds to God's question with another question that I mentioned earlier. He said, " 'Does Job fear God for nothing? . . . Have you not put a hedge around him and his household and everything he has? You have blessed the work of his hands, so that his flocks and herds are spread throughout the land. But stretch out your hand and strike everything he has, and he will surely curse you to your face' " (Job 1:9–10 NIV).

"Does Job fear God for nothing?" The Hebrew word for "nothing" means devoid of cost, reason, or advantage. In other words, Satan is saying, "Does Job fear God without an ulterior purpose?"[2]

Satan is challenging Job's motives. The devil thinks it's foolish to serve God, and when he finds someone who does, he is immediately suspicious of his motives.

Of course Job serves You, the devil reasons. Look what You have given him. A man would be a fool not to serve You because it pays so well. But if serving You were no longer profitable, if You should take everything away from him, then You would see Job for what he really is. He would curse You to Your face.

Satan told the truth about one thing: God had blessed Job. He had seven thousand sheep, three thousand camels, five hundred yoke of oxen, five hundred donkeys, and a large number of servants, plus seven sons and three daughters. He was the greatest man among all the people of the East.

And here we find the theme of the book of Job. It is not, "Why do the righteous suffer?" It is *Why do the righteous serve God?*

Job serves God for what he can get out of Him, Satan claims. Anyone would be willing to worship God under those conditions. But cut off the profit, and Job will renounce You.

You might say Satan had my churchmember's number; I suppose if God had delivered his son from prison, the father would have been in church the following Sunday morning, praising God. But he wouldn't praise God for nothing.

But before I criticize that father, I must answer the question myself: Why do I worship God? It's a fair question. Do I worship God because He is God or because He blesses me with good gifts? What if He stopped "blessing" me? What if He took away the gifts? Let's be honest: It's easy to be good when you have the goods.[3]

When we launch the Stewardship Drive to raise the budget, we tell the people that if they tithe God will bless them, He will make the 90 percent go farther than the 100 percent. But what if He doesn't? What if the only thing you had after you tithed was 10 percent less than you had before you tithed? What if the IRS decreed that gifts to the church were no longer deductible?

Behind Satan's challenge lies a broader question: Is true worship, true piety, possible? Is total and unqualified human allegiance to God, with no strings attached, no qualifiers, no conditions set (such as, I promise to reward you), possible?

Job becomes a victim of a wager made in heaven. Satan throws down the guantlet and makes God the wager. "I'll bet You," the devil says, "that if You stretch out Your hand and strike everything he has, he will curse You to Your face."

God picks up the gauntlet and takes the bet. By doing so, He is saying that Job serves God for Himself, not for His rewards. "Very well, then, everything he has is in your hands, but on the man himself do not lay a finger" (Job 1:12).

Now, by all that we consider just and fair, this is not just, this is not fair. Remember this; we'll come back to it later.

And so it begins. "Will a person serve God for nothing?" Since Job is a book built of questions upon questions, we will discover the answer by asking questions.

The first question is: Will a person serve God when life turns tragic?

CHAPTER
12

WHEN LIFE TURNS TRAGIC

When our son died, we received scores of cards and letters expressing sympathy and support. We treasured every one of them. But I remember one in particular. It was a letter from a couple who were members of a church I had been in recently. The first paragraph contained the usual words of condolence. But it is the second paragraph I remember.

They wrote, "Brother Dunn, we know that you are a man of God and that you and your wife have committed your lives to serving Him. We don't understand how something like this could happen to *you*" (my emphasis).

They could understand something like that happening to them; they were mere people. But I was special, I was a man of God. I believe they were thinking, "If something like *this* can happen to a man of God, what might happen to *us*?"

"We don't understand how something like this could happen to you." And do you know what? I agreed with them.

The truth is, I felt I deserved better treatment. My position ought to merit some consideration. After all, if a person is living for God that ought to count for something, shouldn't it? I mean, there should be some fringe benefits, right? A few perks to go with the job? Special treatment, preferential consideration? Hey, I'm a child of God. I've devoted my life to serving Him—He ought to keep that in mind when He starts handing out calamities and catastrophes. That's only fair.

Fair. That's all I ask, Lord. Just be fair. Is that too much to ask? How can it be fair when the children of my friends are graduating from college, starting careers, getting married, having children while my son lies in a grave? A little justice, Lord.

A little justice.

I've been watching the Great Flood of '93 on television. That Old Man River has really been rolling a lot of tragedy into a lot of lives. Reporters have been talking about the levees and showing dramatic pictures of the raging Mississippi breaking through the levees and flooding the countryside and the cities. One network showed a farmer and his wife waterskiing over their flooded soybean field.

"We spent millions of dollars building these levees," said a mayor of one flooded city. "We trusted them to keep back the flood, but they gave way."

Me too, brother. I trusted in the levees of faith and prayer to keep back the flood waters of tragedy, but they gave way. Or so it seemed at the time.

To change the metaphor, I always thought of faith as a buffer, a cushion that would protect me from the sharp edges of life. But when one of those sharp edges penetrated my faith and pierced my flesh—that's when the questions began. That's when I made the shattering discovery: *You can trust God and still get hurt.*

And that's when you begin to discover what kind of faith you have, because there is one thing both God and

Satan agree on: Faith that depends upon prosperity is not genuine. Satan's challenge is legitimate.[1]

What happened to Job is unbelievable (and undeserved) tragedy. One day an exhausted and frightened messenger brings news that rustlers have stolen the donkeys and oxen and killed all his servants. Only the messenger escaped.

While the first messenger is still speaking, another bursts through the door to tell Job that fire fell from heaven and consumed the sheep and the servants. Only the messenger escaped.

Before Job has time to digest this report, another messenger rushes in with the terrible news that a tornado has killed his sons and daughters. Only the messenger escaped.

I think if I had been Job I would have said, "I'm going to shoot the next person that comes through that door!"

But do you know what Job did? He fell to the ground and worshiped God. Listen:

> "Naked I came from my mother's womb,
>   and naked I will depart.
> The LORD gave and the LORD has taken away;
>   may the name of the LORD be praised."
>
> (Job 1:21)

And then comes one of the most astounding statements in all the Bible: "In all this, Job did not sin by charging God with wrongdoing" (Job 1:22).

THE STAKES ARE RAISED

God has won the first round.

Satan must have been furious. But he doesn't give up. Once again he appears before God, and once again the

Lord boasts of Job's piety. And once again Satan impugns Job's faithfulness.

" 'Skin for skin!' Satan replied. 'A man will give all he has for his own life. But stretch out your hand and strike his flesh and bones, and he will surely curse you to your face'" (Job 2:4–5).

And once again, God accepts the challenge. "Very well, then, he is in your hands; but you must spare his life" (Job 2:6). Why spare Job's life? Because you won't know who won the wager if he dies. The dead cannot praise the Lord.

The result? Job, sitting on an ash heap, covered with painful sores, scraping himself with a piece of broken pottery, his wife urging him to curse God and die. "Are you still holding on to your integrity?" she mocks (Job 2:9).

And can you believe Job's response? " 'You are talking like a foolish woman. Shall we accept good from God and not trouble?' In all this, Job did not sin in what he said" (Job 2:10).

Amazing.

Will a person serve God when his or her storybook life turns tragic? I am using the words *tragic* and *tragedy* in the literary sense to distinguish between what some theologians call radical suffering and "regular" suffering.

John Barbour depicts tragedy as:

the downfall of a good man or woman. "A good man" is a person with a particular kind of moral excellence, somebody who embodies his culture's idea of virtue. Despite his moral goodness, the protagonist of a tragedy suffers or dies in an unusually disturbing way. A central theme of tragic literature is that human virtue does not suffice for happiness because of the possibility of tragic error. In fact, it is often as a consequence of his most morally admirable actions that a character makes a tragic error and suffers his fate; a less virtuous individual would have escaped disaster. The very virtue of the central figure, then, contributes to his downfall.[2]

Radical suffering (tragedy) is suffering that degrades, dehumanizes, and destroys the human spirit and it is suffering that cannot be traced to punishment or understood as something deserved (like the death of a child).[3]

BEWITCHED, BOTHERED, AND BEWILDERED

Job is suffering precisely because he is a good man. He discovered that you can serve God perfectly and still suffer. And it is exactly this that makes his affliction such a puzzle—he doesn't deserve it.

If Job had been a great sinner, we would say, "Well, there is justice in the world after all. Old Job is getting exactly what he deserves." Or if he had been just an average person, we could say, "Boy, Job really had a bad day. But that's life. Some people are luckier than others."

There would be no problem if Job were wicked, but when the guy is perfect. . . . But this, of course, has always been one of the strongest arguments against the existence of God: Why do bad things happen to good people? Everyone knows that the good should be happy, but human morality does not guarantee happiness in this life. Nor does happiness necessarily produce a moral life.[4]

THE REAL PROBLEM

Job's suffering cannot be reduced simply to the loss of his possessions and children or even to his own physical pain. There was a greater source of anguish.

Job realized that the orthodox doctrine he had believed all his life was false. His theology broke down under the strain of the facts.

The prevailing theology of that day was simple: God blessed the righteous and cursed the unrighteous. Physical and material blessings (health and wealth) were indisputable evidence of God's favor. Loss of health and wealth were indisputable evidence of God's displeasure.

But Job knew in his heart he was innocent; he had not done anything to explain the magnitude of his suffering. And yet he could not deny what was happening. Suddenly everything that he had believed, everything that had given his life order and meaning, everything he thought he knew about God collapsed in a cloud of dust.

No greater crisis can befall a person. All our life, whether consciously or unconsciously, we build an inner system of belief, belief in a universe of order and justice ruled over by the One who created it. And when this inner fortress, which comforts us with its security, is destroyed, our life turns into a meaningless mess—unless we can penetrate the mystery and bring back an explanation that will restore meaning. And in Job's day that explanation was sin.

Fortunately, that kind of theology is no longer with us, right?

Wrong.

I remember a ministry newsletter I received not long ago in which the preacher said, "Your financial condition is a reflection of your spiritual condition." (Interestingly, the same day I received a promotional letter—the kind where sentences are underlined in blue—from the same preacher, pleading for money to pay the bills.)

This is, of course, absolute nonsense. Just as are the efforts of those who try to prove that Jesus and His disciples were rich!

The truth is that we all feel guilty when things go wrong. A mother stands beside the sickbed of her child and whispers, "God is punishing me." She doesn't know for what, but she knows it's for something. A man watches his business go down the tube, and he wonders what sin he committed.

I have an idea you have experienced something like this or you would not have picked up this book in the first place. Perhaps it's "normal" to feel that our suffering is the result of some sin in our life. And there is no lack of people willing to affirm us in that confession. But such people actually side with the devil and Job's three friends when they tell us we need to "have more faith" or to "confess our sin."

But back to Job. Like him, when our life turns tragic and we face the mystery of why we are suffering, we are forced into new ways of thinking and speaking about God. Will we continue to serve Him anyway?

Ah Lord, had You but kept silent, Job would not have suffered. What are You saying now that is causing me to suffer? Why do You speak to my Adversary and not to me, Your child?

I have been daily grateful for the friend who remarked that grief isolates. He did not mean only that I, grieving, am isolated from you, happy. He meant also that *shared* grief isolates the sharers from each other. Though united in that we are grieving, we grieve differently. As each death has its own character, so too each grief over a death has its own character—its own escape. The dynamics of each person's sorrow must be allowed to work themselves out without judgment. I may find it strange that you should be tearful today but dry-eyed yesterday when my tears were yesterday. But my sorrow is not your sorrow.

There's something more: I must struggle so hard to regain life that I cannot reach out to you. Nor you to me. The one not grieving must touch us both. It's when people are happy that they say, "Let's get together."

Nicholas Wolterstorff, *Lament for a Son*

CHAPTER
13

WHEN WE MUST STAND ALONE

A few weeks ago Kaye and I sat in a restaurant eating lunch with a minister and his wife. For the past several years the wife had been suffering from severe manic depression. As we talked it became obvious that the pain of her illness had been exacerbated by the attitude of friends and colleagues. She carried, as do most victims of depression, a double burden. Not only must she contend with a crippling illness but also with the public branding and rejection. I remembered reading that *stigma* was the single most destructive factor in the care and recovery of persons with mental illness.[1] And I recalled that a few weeks before our son's death, I was invited by a Christian psychologist who was holding conferences across the country on the family, to join him as a speaker in the conferences. After Ronnie committed suicide, I didn't hear from him again.

As the minister's wife struggled to describe the sometimes bizarre episodes of her depression, Kaye would nod and say, "Yes, Ronnie, Jr. was like that. Ronnie, Jr. did that too."

Suddenly she nearly leaped out of the booth, her eyes wide and excited, an expression of glorious relief on her face: "You understand!" she shouted. "You understand!"

I was amazed because this seemed to be enough. We offered no answers, no solutions. She had not asked for any—all she asked for was understanding—and when she found someone who understood, she was no longer alone.

Someone to say, "I understand."

That's more than Job had.

The fifth and crowning disaster to fall upon Job was a hideous leprosy-like disease, which was considered a singular sign of divine displeasure. Not only was Job in intense physical pain, but he was also now a social outcast, reduced to sitting on the burnt dung-heaps outside of town, scraping his sores with a piece of broken pottery.

That's where his wife found him.

And she said to him, "Are you still holding on to your integrity? Curse God and die!" (Job 2:9).

No understanding there.

News of Job's plight soon reached his three best friends, Eliphaz, Bildad, and Zophar, and they came to comfort him. But when they saw him they were horrified at his condition; they cried aloud and wept and tore their clothes and threw dust into the air.

Ah, at last. Understanding. Sympathy.

And then the three friends sat down on the ground and watched him for seven days and seven nights without saying a word.

After sitting there for seven days, like vultures perched on a limb waiting for the dying to die, they spoke.

Eliphaz said: "It is your sin that has attracted the wrath of God."

Bildad said: "God does not make mistakes. God knows your sin even if you do not."

Zophar said: "Who are you to question the ways of God? You are suffering for your sins."

So much for the comfort of friends. So much for understanding.

But, of course, they accused him. They had to; they had no choice. Champions of the fixed mind, they value orthodoxy more than truth. They are fighting for their religious lives. *Their* "fear of God" and the "integrity of *their* ways" is at stake. A suffering Job, a suffering *righteous* man called their theology into question. "Their only defense is to deny their friend and turn from him, and if the denial of one human life is the price they must pay to preserve their theological structure, then so be it."[2]

So desperate are we to preserve this theological structure that we will go to any lengths to discover a fault in Job that brought about his disastrous condition, in spite of the thrice made claim, once by the writer and twice by God Himself that Job is blameless.

Ignoring the fact that in 2:3 God states clearly that He is ruining Job "without any reason" (that's pretty strong language for those with a zippity-do-da kind of faith), many seize upon Job's lament in 3:25 that "What I had feared has come upon me, what I dreaded has happened to me." "Aha!" exclaim these modern friends of Job. "There's the culprit—fear! If Job had not feared those things he would not have suffered!"

Aside from the fact that the Bible does not accept that explanation, such rationalization leads to fear itself—fear that in some unguarded moment a word or a thought will condemn them to disaster. What parent has never, even for the thinnest of moments, feared the death of a child?

This is a doctrine of superstition resulting in bondage to Satan rather than freedom in Christ.

God insists that what is happening to Job is "without any reason." Of course, there was a reason—on God's side. But as far as Job was concerned, there was no reason.

Those who refuse to accept this fact are no better than Job's three friends, who came to comfort, but stayed to criticize, and whom God later rebuked for their words. As one writer has said:

> "Human frames of meaning are limited and at best partial, and interpreters of Job must face this as well. Tragedy is not for those who cannot accept unanswered and unanswerable questions, or answers that are questions. Nor is it for those who will not question. EASY ANSWERS DENY JOB THE RECOGNITION AND SYMPATHY HIS SUFFERING AND INTEGRITY DEMAND."[3]

FROM THE CITY COUNCIL TO THE CITY DUMP

It's a long way that Job has come. A long way from the days when friends crowded around him, flattered him, sought his advice and listened to his counsel. A long way from the warmth of an understanding wife and the love of devoted children. Once he stood surrounded by myriad friends and loved ones cheering him on.

Now he stands alone. Rather, he sits alone. But, having lost everything else, he refuses to let go of his integrity.

There is a progression in Job's suffering. First, his suffering is tragic, without meaning, without understanding. Like Joseph K., the protagonist in Kafka's *The Trial*, Job has been arrested, tried, and convicted without ever hearing the charges against him.

And now this second phase, misunderstood by and thus abandoned by his friends. Listen as he lashes out at these comfortless comforters:

"A despairing man should have the devotion of his friends, even though he forsakes the fear of the Almighty.

"But my brothers are as undependable as intermittent streams, as the streams that overflow

"When darkened by thawing ice and swollen with melting snow,

But that cease to flow in the dry season, and in the heat vanish from their channels. . . .

"They are distressed, because they had been confident; they arrive there, only to be disappointed.

"Now you too have proved to be of no help; you see something dreadful and are afraid." (Job 6:14–17, 20, 21)

ISOLATION

All suffering has a tendency to isolate, whether it is mental or physical, a wayward child, a crumbling marriage, or a failing business. You live in a different world of sounds and colors and interests. You are defined by your plight; it touches and shapes every moment of your existence. It casts its shadow over each part of your daily life. Cynthia Swindoll summarizes her fifteen-year struggle with depression in these words: "Depression . . . black as a thousand midnights in a cypress swamp. Loneliness that is indescribable. Confusion regarding God. Frustration with life and circumstances. The feeling that you have been abandoned, that you are worthless. Unloveable. The pain is excruciating."[4]

Sometimes this isolation from others occurs because God is working in our life in a different way, an unusual, perhaps even an unconventional way. So different, so unconventional, they can see it only as judgment or chastisement. Having deduced the ways of God's workings, when they see that pattern challenged by the experience of another, they can draw only one conclusion, for they are champions of the fixed mind.

Like Job's friends, in order to defend their vision, they must deny the integrity of the sufferer.

So Job sits on his ashheap, an outcast.

LONELINESS

Isolation leads to loneliness. Joseph Conrad said that people must suffer as they dream—alone. Because Job's three friends do not understand his trouble, their presence only accentuates his loneliness. It has been suggested that the most terrible early experience of an individual is loneliness, and that loneliness may be the greatest pain in suffering.[5]

A woman whose husband has died in a plane crash sits Sunday morning in the midst of a singing, joyful, clapping congregation of worshipers—and sits alone. The joy of the worshipers only heightens her sense of loss and increasing loneliness. She will not return for the evening service, for she resents their exuberant camaraderie. She is one of the authors of Psalm 42:

> These things I remember
>   as I pour out my soul:
> how I used to go with the multitude,
>   leading the procession to the house of God,
> with shouts of joy and thanksgiving
>   among the festive throng. (v. 4)

But the greatest loneliness is not caused by the isolation from family, friends, and society, but by the suspicion that you have been abandoned by God. Which is how Job was beginning to feel just about now. And which, in his case (and often ours), turned to bitterness.

BITTERNESS

The loneliness expressed in chapter 6 gives way to the bitterness of chapter 7. Isolation . . . loneliness . . . bitterness—that is the sequence of unresolved suffering. Bitterness at the God who is the cause of pain and suffering.

> What is man that you make so
>   much of him,
> that you give him so much
>   attention,
> that you examine him every
>   morning
> and test him every moment?
> Will you never look away from me,
>   or let me alone even for an
>   instant? . . .
> Why have you made me your
>   target? (Job 7:17–20)

Can you believe that Job is speaking to God in this way? It reminds us that the book of Job is not a book of passive submission, but one of active protest. And as we will see later, the psalms show us that such speech is proper in the presence of God.

The striking feature of these words is that Job is complaining of God's presence, not His absence. God is too close for comfort. Bitterness perceives the presence of God an oppressive presence.[6]

It comes as a surprise to the modern reader that Job never expresses doubt in the existence of God. Contemporary sufferers often solve the mystery of their pain by denying either God's existence or His sovereignty. Job denies neither.

For Job, the issue is never "Does God exist?" or "Is God sovereign?" The issue is the *character* of God. What kind of

God is this who treats His faithful friend like an enemy? Job's name may even mean "enemy."[7]

When C. S. Lewis was doing battle with the ways of God during his wife's terminal illness, he put his thoughts into these words: "Not that I am (I think) in much danger of ceasing to believe in God. The real danger is of coming to believe such dreadful things about Him. The conclusion I dread is not, 'So there's no God after all,' but, 'So this is what God's really like. Deceive yourself no longer.'"[8]

And so the question stands: "Will a person serve God when he must stand alone?" Or to put it more bluntly, "Will I remain faithful to God even though it appears God is no longer faithful to me?"

One of my best friends, Manley Beasley, died in 1990. I guess the only thing that surprised his many friends is that he lived as long as he did. Stricken in 1970 by five serious diseases, three of which were terminal, Manley spent the next twenty years on life-support systems—not the medical kind, but the spiritual kind. Jesus literally became his life. In Manley's words, he was alive by His life. There must have been a dozen or more times in those twenty years when Manley came to the brink of death only to come back, stronger than before. I remember going to hospitals at least six times to say good-bye to him because the doctors said he wouldn't make it through the night. I said to him once, "You're the hardest man to say good-bye to I've ever known." Yet, in spite of his physical condition, he carried on a worldwide ministry and taught thousands what it means to walk by faith.

The next to the last time Manley was hospitalized he was confined for several months to the intensive care unit. When Kaye and I visited him in the hospital we were certain it was the last time we would see him. You can imagine our surprise, therefore, while we were away in

Georgia, to learn that Manley had once again astonished everyone, including his doctors, by living.

I called him at his home, and we talked for a long time. After our conversation, I wrote him this letter. It's dated November 4, 1988.

Dear Manley:

Our phone conversation a few minutes ago spoke to my heart in several ways. God has been so good to grant us the desires of our hearts—namely, to keep you here. I believe your greatest ministry lies before you, and few people will ever realize what it cost.

I have been for some time immersing myself in that great passage in Romans 8:31–39, and I am being forced to rethink my idea of "victory." Paul enumerates all the evils and the not-so-evils that threaten us, and he says that in all these things we are more than conquerors—supra-conquerors is the word. It means to go beyond and above mere conquest. In the midst of these things we do more than conquer; we go beyond that to something greater and better. It is not necessarily deliverance from famine and slaughter that demonstrates divine victory. The Marines could save us from slaughter, and the Red Cross could save us from famine.

In verse 35 Paul lists things that are evil, catastrophic: "tribulation, or distress, or persecution, or famine, or nakedness, or peril, or sword. . . ."

And then in verse 38 he names things that are good, natural, or neutral: death, life, angels (not fallen angels), nor principalities, nor powers, nor things present, nor things to come, nor height, nor depth, nor any other created thing—these things are forces of everyday life, neither good nor necessarily bad, but neutral.

Now what do both categories of powers try to do to us? They try to separate us from the love of God. This is surprising. I would speak of the pain, the suffering they inflict, the danger of death, the fear, the terror they bring to our hearts. But Paul does not say that the conquest consists in escaping these things, nor in their removal. To Paul, the conquest is that even the most horrible of powers and events "cannot separate us from the love of God which is in Christ Jesus."

What is the *greatest* exhibition of the power of God? Not to remove the pain or take away the slaughter, but to keep us in the love of God through it all.

Now my point: *The despair of the sufferer is not caused by the depth of the suffering but by the depth of his sense of separation from God.*

You said that when you were finally able to get hold of God, the peace came. The suffering didn't diminish, it was as deep as ever, but the sense of separation had vanished. You no longer felt separated from God.

On the cross Jesus never cried out about the pain of the nails or the agony of the sword or the shame of the nakedness. This was His despair: "My God, My God, why hast Thou forsaken Me?"

I believe it is true that the fear and despair I feel lying on a hospital bed, not knowing if I will live or die, is caused, not by the pain or the fear of dying, but by the fact that I seem to have lost contact with God. I can't sense His presence, I can't get hold of Him. But when I do, the sense of separation from God is dispelled; the despair, the fear is relieved. The pain may remain, but the despair does not. It is not the suffering but the separation that undermines our confidence in God.

What do you think?

In the Best of Bonds,
Ron

Well, what do *you* think?

I think Teilhard de Chardin was right: *Joy is not the absence of pain but the presence of God.*

114

CHAPTER
14

WHEN GOD IS SILENT

Silence can be a terrifying thing.

Especially to a fifth-grader.

Miss Meyers had left the classroom, and all thirty of her students were making the most of her absence, even though she had sentenced us to civilized behavior. We were giggling, chattering, throwing spit balls, scraping Depression-era chewing gum from under the desks and hurling it across the room—civilized behavior for fifth-graders. I was turned around in my seat with my back to the door, unloading spit balls at a guy two rows away, when the room suddenly exploded with silence. Everything went quiet, like someone had thrown a switch. It was the most terrifying thing I had ever not heard. I knew what it meant—and it was not good news. I slowly turned around, avoiding Miss Meyers's glowering eyes, and spent the rest of the afternoon in the hall.

I am reminded of the first verse in the eighth chapter of Revelation: "When he opened the seventh seal, there was silence in heaven for about half an hour." Silence before wrath.

The silence of God can be a terrifying thing. The feeling of separation we talked about in the last chapter is intensified when God remains silent. From his ash-heap, Job demands that God read the charges against him. Surely he has the right to know for what crime he is being punished.

The silence of God is suspicious. Like a witness who pleads the fifth, God's silence is interpreted as guilty silence. For Job the question is no longer his innocence, but *God's* innocence. Can a person who suffers undeservedly continue to believe that a silent God is a just God?

And so Job indicts God. He determines the questions to be answered. He demands that God justify His actions.

But heaven is silent. A first reader of Job may be surprised that God does not explain to Job why he is suffering. As a matter of fact, when it is all over, Job still does not know why he has suffered. He is never informed of the conversation in heaven between God and Satan. He never learns of the wager.

There are many wounded people who will live out their days and die without knowing why tragedy interrupted their lives. If only God would say something. All I'm asking for, Lord, is some clue as to why all these things happened. I could make it if You would speak to me. Just a hint, Lord, just a hint, okay?

But, like Job, we learn the tough lesson that God is not obligated to explain His actions. Humans need a system of justice; God does not. God sets the standards of human behavior, but He Himself is not bound by them unless He chooses to be.

THE SILENCE IS BROKEN

But God does speak, finally. At last, some answers! It's about time. After thirty-seven chapters of silence, we're going to hear God's side of the story.

Let's listen. Out of the whirlwind God speaks:

"Who is this that darkens my counsel
    with words without knowledge?
Brace yourself like a man;
    I will question you,
    and you shall answer me." (Job 38:2–3)

Freely translated, God is saying, "Job, you don't have a clue as to what's going on. Fasten your seat belt, son. It's time for you to answer some questions."

I get the feeling this is not going to go the way Job expects. But at least God is talking.

"Where were you when I laid the earth's foundation?
Tell me, if you understand.
Who marked off its dimensions? Surely you know!
Who stretched a measuring line across it?"
                        (Job 38:4–5)

Wait a minute. God isn't answering questions, He's asking them. And what He is saying is totally irrelevant; it has nothing to do with what's been going on. God acts like a judge who dozes off in the middle of a trial—He's missed the main argument.

GOD HAS A RIGHT

When at long last God speaks, He tells Job to turn on the Discovery Channel. He tells him to take a nature hike. He flings the universe in Job's face and invites the creature to instruct the Creator.

What is God saying? He's saying that He has a right to do what He does. God alone, who has created and comprehended the vast universe, has the right to govern and the right to say whether He is governing it properly.

And this is the first, and perhaps the most difficult, hurdle of all. We will never be able to live with life's disappointments unless we settle this issue.

To meet God is not to get answers to our questions; it is to learn the right questions. And the right question here is "Does God have a right to do what He does?"

This is the first question I had to face the night we learned of Ronnie, Jr.'s death. On his gravemarker are these words from Psalm 115:3: "But our God is in the heavens: he hath done whatsoever he hath pleased." This is the verse that came immediately to mind that night.

GOD HAS A REASON

Then Job replied to the Lord:

> "I know that you can do all things;
> no plan of yours can be thwarted."
> (Job 42:1–2)

There is a purpose, Job says. I may not know what that purpose is, but it is enough to know that there is one.

And this is one of the supreme lessons of the book of Job: Our suffering serves some larger purpose of God. "This links our human lives with a divine purpose, just at the point where the purposes of God seem broken off. Pain is transformed into privilege; sorrow becomes the sign of divine approval."[1]

GOD HAS A REWARD

One last thing the author of Job wants us to learn—God has a reward.

"After Job had prayed for his friends, the LORD made him prosperous again and gave him twice as much as he had before.... The LORD blessed the latter part of Job's life more than the first" (Job 42:10, 12, NIV).

All of his relatives and friends threw Job a party, and they brought gifts—a piece of silver and a gold ring.

I love these words, "The Lord blessed the latter part of Job's life more than the first." I believe that is what God wants to do for all of us. He always saves the best wine until last.

Well, let's see how God rewarded Job. Remember that He gave Job twice as much as he had before. And then comes the inventory.

He had fourteen thousand sheep; he started with seven thousand.

He had six thousand camels; he started with three thousand.

He had a thousand yoke of oxen; he started with five hundred.

He had a thousand donkeys; he started with five hundred.

He had seven sons and three daughters; he started with seven and three. Wait, I must have read that wrong. He had seven sons and three daughters.... No, that can't be right. He started out with ten children, now he ought to have twenty. I must be reading from a liberal translation.

It says the same thing in your Bible, too? Hum.

Wait, I get it! He did have twenty children. Ten down here and ten in heaven. Because you never lose someone when they go to heaven.

Dr. Vance Havner was a traveling preacher for forty years. He didn't marry until he was forty—said he wanted to think about it first. He never learned to drive a car. But his wife, Sara, drove them to his meetings in the Buick when they didn't fly or ride the train. The two of them were inseparable. Until 1973, when Sara died.

Occasionally someone would say to Dr. Havner afterward, "I hear you lost your wife."

"No," Dr. Havner would say, "I didn't lose her. I know right where she is. You haven't lost someone if you know where they are."

And then he would quote this poem:

> Death can hide but not divide;
> She is but on Christ's other side.
> She with Christ and Christ with me,
> United still in Christ are we.

One final observation: The Lord told Eliphaz that He was angry with him and his two friends because they had not spoken properly of Him as Job had. God commanded them to make sacrifices for themselves. "My servant Job will pray for you, and I will accept his prayer and not deal with you according to your folly."

Isn't that a nice touch? *Those who suffer deeply can also save.*

I like to imagine that God went looking for Satan afterward. Satan probably made himself scarce. God probably found him hiding behind a bush. "Come on out, Satan, and pay up. I won the bet. I told you Job would serve Me for nothing, and I was right."

I like to imagine that maybe someday God could point to me and say to Satan, "See, I told you he would serve Me for nothing."

Part Three: What to Do When You Don't Know What to Do—
The Ministry of Darkness

Two evils, monstrous either one apart,
Possessed me, and were long and loath at going;
A cry of Absence, Absence, in the heart,
And in the wood the furious winter blowing.

John Crowe Ransom

A religion that does not affirm that God is hidden
is not true.

Pascal

Who among you fears the LORD
   and obeys the word of his servant?
Let him who walks in the dark,
   who has no light,
trust in the name of the LORD
   and rely on his God.

Isaiah 50:10

CHAPTER
15

THE DARK SIDE OF GRACE

A few years ago I sat in a motel room with four men, whom I considered some of the godliest people I knew, discussing with a publisher what we believed were some of the needs among Christians that needed to be addressed. The topics ranged from prayer and personal Bible study to marriage and home life. Nothing new there, really.

Then we broke for lunch, and everyone relaxed and started talking "off the record." In a sudden burst of honesty, all four men confessed to a present spiritual darkness in their lives. One admitted he had not "felt God's presence in six months." Others talked about their inability to pray and their lack of confidence in what they were doing. They were carrying on, of course, preaching on Sundays, visiting the sick, witnessing to the lost, doing everything expected of them as ministers. But they were doing it without any sense of God's presence. It had become so bad for one that he had begun to doubt his salvation. This, he said, was hard to admit, even to himself, since he had just written a highly successful book on the Christian life.

In a word, all of these men were walking in darkness. This was good news to me because I thought I was the only one who felt like that.

When we gathered after lunch, we all agreed that this subject ought to be addressed, for if we were experiencing this, surely others were too. But nothing was done about it. It was an unmarketable subject.

AN INEVITABLE AND LEGITIMATE EXPERIENCE?

Darkness, despair, depression—are these legitimate spiritual experiences? Isaiah the prophet thought so: "Who among you fears the LORD / and obeys the word of his servant? / Let him who walks in the dark, / who has no light, / trust in the name of the LORD / and rely on his God" (Isa. 50:10).

As a matter of fact, Isaiah is saying that the way you can recognize one who fears God and obeys the Lord Jesus is by observing how he acts in the darkness.

The picture Isaiah portrays is that of a man on a journey. As he walks, the light is suddenly withdrawn and darkness rushes in. The Hebrew text indicates that "he walks in deep darkness without even a glimmer of light to guide him." When there is light, you know where you are, you can see where you're going, you can read the road signs and know how far it is to the end of your journey. When there is light you see obstacles in the road, you can distinguish friend from foe. When there is light, there is knowledge, there is assurance.

In the darkness you have none of these things. You feel alone, abandoned, forsaken. Theologians have a term for this: *Deus Absconditus*—the God who is hidden. Richard Foster calls it the "Sahara of the heart."[1] John of the Cross described it as the "dark night of the soul."

The Dark Night of the Soul—when no light is thrown on the "why?" of your suffering; when the usual means of grace—prayer, worship, singing, God's Word—have no effect on the drooping spirit; when you are "numb" to spiritual things; when the tried and true formulas from books and seminars sound hollow and empty; when you discover there are some things you cannot praise or pray your way out of. You can rebuke the devil, plead the blood, station angels, and wear garlic around your neck, but nothing moves the darkness.

THE PLOT THICKENS AND THE DARKNESS DEEPENS

This "dark night of the soul" is, as I have stated, an inevitable and legitimate experience of the believer. It is not "a rabbit trail but a major highway."[2] Saints through the ages have trod this dark road before us. In fact, it's a major theme of many of the psalms.

> How long, O LORD? Will you forget me forever?
>   How long will you hide your face from me?
> (Ps. 13:1)

> My soul thirsts for God, for the living God.
>   When can I go and meet with God?
> My tears have been my food day and night,
> while men say to me all day long,
>   "Where is your God?"
> . . . .
> Why are you downcast, O my soul?
>   Why so disturbed within me?

. . . .
I say to God my Rock,
   "Why have you forgotten me?
Why must I go about mourning,
   oppressed by the enemy?" (Ps. 42:2–3, 5, 9)

And there are many others, both personal and communal: Psalms 22; 25; 39; 86; 88; 109; to mention just a few. Actually, there are nearly as many psalms of lament, protest, and complaint as there are of praise and thanksgiving. But we do not hear much about them.

And that is strange because we think of the psalms as the hymnbook of the Church. Right now there is a sweeping revival of psalm-singing in many churches, ignited by a new emphasis on praise.

Why don't we ever sing Psalm 88? I'll tell you why. Listen:

O LORD, the God who saves me,
   day and night I cry out before you.
May my prayer come before you;
   turn your ear to my cry. (vv. 1–2)

Now here's his prayer, his cry:

For my soul is full of trouble
   and my life draws near the grave.
I am counted among those who go down to the pit;
   I am like a man without strength.
I am set apart with the dead,
   like the slain who lie in the grave,
whom you remember no more,
   who are cut off from your care. (vv. 3–5)

It gets worse:

You have put me in the lowest pit,
  in the darkest depths.
Your wrath lies heavily upon me;
  you have overwhelmed me with all your waves.
You have taken from me my closest friends
  and have made me repulsive to them.
I am confined and cannot escape;
  my eyes are dim with grief. (vv. 6–9)

Had enough? Let's skip to the conclusion—maybe it turns out all right in the end.

From my youth I have been afflicted and close to death.
  I have suffered your terrors and am in despair.
Your wrath has swept over me;
  your terrors have destroyed me.
All day long they surround me like a flood;
  they have completely engulfed me.
You have taken my companions and loved ones from me;
  the darkness is my closest friend. (vv. 15–18)

Try throwing that on your overhead this Sunday morning and see what it does to your praise service.

No, I'm not advocating that. It's too depressing.

But it *is* real.

I know it's real, because it is in the Bible, I have experienced it, and I counsel believers every week who are struggling through the experience and could honestly say, "The darkness is my closest friend."

The bravest seek me out after the services. I see them out of the corner of my eye. They won't approach me until I'm alone, until I'm finished greeting people and shaking hands. Some give up and leave. But others stay, lingering on the fringes of the crowd. When I'm alone, they come, with furtive glances; they speak guarded words in whispered tones from a dry mouth. The darkness is their closest friend.

They are outsiders because they have an unspiritual affliction. They are an embarrassment to the other members of the Church of the Feeling Good. They are reluctant to admit to the darkness for fear they will hear the same admonitions: "Pull yourself together." "Confess your sins." "Die to self." "Crucify the flesh." "Count your blessings." "Be thankful you don't have cancer."

Some, I think, would be willing to exchange their darkness for cancer. At least then they could acknowledge the pain and get help and find comfort.

SEASONS OF THE SOUL

Writing after the death of his first wife, Martin E. Marty, in *A Cry of Absence*, talks about the wintry season of the heart, the frigid cold blasts that come in the wake of pain or death—an absence in the heart. "Wintry frost comes in the void left when a love dies or a lover grows distant. . . . The absence can also come, however, to a waste space left when the divine is distant, the sacred is remote, when God is silent."[3]

Winter, Marty insists, is just as legitimate a season of the soul as is summer and spring. But it finds little help or understanding. In the current religious atmosphere, only brightly lit summer spirituality is allowed.

Picture someone hungry for a warming of the spirit. He calls a friend who is advertised as spirit-filled. "Praise the Lord!" she responds, as she picks up the telephone. The two meet in person. One is chilly but open to stirrings, the other well characterized as full of stir. What transfer of spirit can occur when the filled person is compulsive about the summer and sunshine in her heart. Never does a frown cloud her face. Lips, once drawn tight in disapproval, are now tight in a cosmetic smile. "The Lord wills it." Never does the storm of the troubled heart receive its chance to be heard. The Lord has satisfied every need, one hears, so it would be sin to stare once more at the void within. Christ is the answer, the spirit is warm and no chill is ever allowed between the boards or around the windows of the soul.[4]

But Marty carries this idea further when he says, "Maybe, one thinks, the summery kind of spirituality has less to do with the Spirit than with personality types, social classes, income groups, and patterns of etiquette. Not every believer can move easily into the rhythms of country-and-western Christianity with its foot-stomping, exuberant styles. Those styles may come naturally and be authentic to people in some regions and ranks. *Must they be the same for everyone?* The suspendered, buttoned-down believer—is he ruled out of the kingdom of warmth because his personality type is restrained, decorous, cool?"[5]

I've quoted Marty at length because I couldn't think of a better way to say it. "Must they [the spiritual styles] be the same for everyone?" he asks. We are deceiving ourselves if we believe that the spiritual styles or expressions must be the same or are the same. They are not. For some, praise is just as real singing "Majestic Sweetness Sits Enthroned Upon the Savior's Brow" as "Clap Your Hands, All Ye People," with the gestures, is to someone else. To say that one is praise and the other is not betrays a shallow understanding of praise.

Must they all be the same? Are we to be conformed to the image of Christ or to the image of one another? Grace does not denaturalize us. Salvation does not dehumanize us. We are in Christ, but in Him we still retain our personality, our individuality. The body, the individual personality, is important to God, for it is the *body* that He will resurrect. Our Lord possesses something now in heaven that He did not have before the incarnation: a body. It was in this recognizable body that Jesus was raised, and in that body He now intercedes for us. And this same Jesus, in the same body, will return to take us to Himself.

I suspect that many "summery" Christians are hiding "wintry" hearts. They deny reality and call it faith. But they will never tell lest they be excommunicated from the Fellowship of the Excited.

SUFFERING AND SILENCE

In some areas of Christianity, silence is considered to be the proper response to suffering. But silence only deepens the darkness. As we observed in the section on Job, suffering has an isolating effect on the sufferer. He sees himself forsaken by God and forgotten by everyone else. To remain silent under the burden of suffering means to become more and more isolated.

But the Scriptures do not encourage silence or forbid speaking. If we learn anything from Job and Jeremiah and David, and even Jesus—who cried out on the cross, "My God, My God! Why have you forsaken me?"—it is that it is right and essential to express the pain of our souls. Sometimes the suffering can be endured only when the pain can be articulated.

> The sufferer himself must find a way to express and identify his suffering; it is not sufficient to have someone speak on his behalf. If people cannot speak about their affliction they will be destroyed by it, or swallowed up by apathy.... Without the capacity to communicate with others there can be no change. To become speechless, to be totally without any relationship, that is death.[6]

130

I learned a valuable and liberating truth in the dark. It's okay to tell God how you feel. After all, He already knows. I've never told God anything He didn't already know. I've never heard God gasp in surprise at anything I said. I've never heard God say in response to any confession, "I would never have believed that of you."

THE ELUSIVE GOD

Israel was constantly grappling with the problem of God's presence and absence. One moment He would be powerfully present and at another absent and hidden. The people had a passion for God's presence, and an integral part of their faith was the belief that God was with them. Yet Isaiah could say, "Truly you are a God who hides himself, O God and Savior of Israel" (Isa. 45:15).

"Israel was repeatedly plagued by the experience of God's hiddenness. Time and again the disparity between religious convictions and the realities of actual experience brought the issue into the forefront of Israel's thought."[7]

Yet what is surprising, and instructive, is that when the Israelites penned their Scriptures they did not deny this experience or seek to hide its reality. This is especially so with the psalms of lament and protest. Why weren't these psalms deleted? If you want to make your faith attractive, not to say marketable, those words would be better unspoken.

Commenting on Psalm 88, Walter Brueggemann asks, "What is a psalm like this doing in our Bible?"[8] It is there, he says, because life is like that, and these poems are intended to speak to all of life, not just part of it. I said earlier this was a depressing psalm, and so it is. But it is an *expressed* psalm. It is not a psalm "of mute depression. It is still speech. It is still addressed. In the bottom of the Pit, Israel still knows it has to do with Yahweh."[9]

In his theological commentary on Psalms, Brueggemann divides them into Psalms of Orientation and Psalms of Disorientation. He finds it curious that the Church, in a world that is increasingly experienced as disoriented, continues to sing almost exclusively songs of orientation. What he says on this matter is so on target, I'm going to quote him at length.

> It is my judgment that this action of the church is less an evangelical defiance guided by faith, and much more a frightened, numb denial and deception that does not want to acknowledge or experience the disorientation of life. The reason for such relentless affirmation of orientation seems to come, not from faith, but from the wishful optimism of our culture.
>
> Such a denial and cover-up, which I take it to be, is an odd inclination for passionate Bible users, given the large number of psalms that are songs of lament, protest, and complaint about the incoherence that is experienced in the world. At least it is clear that a church that goes on singing "happy songs" in the face of raw reality is doing something very different from what the Bible itself does.[10]

Again let me make it clear that I am not suggesting we sing this psalm Sunday morning. I am suggesting that the Church needs to come to grips with the fact that disorientation is a legitimate spiritual experience many of its followers are enduring and that a place needs to be made for them in its ministry.

"The use of these 'psalms of darkness' may be judged by the world to be *acts of unfaith and failure;* but for the trusting community, their use is *an act of bold faith,* albeit a transformed faith. It is an act of bold faith, on the one hand, because it insists that the world must be experienced as it really is and not in some pretended way. On the other hand, it is bold because it insists that all such experiences of disorder are a proper subject for discourse with God. There is nothing out of bounds, nothing precluded or inappropriate. Everything properly belongs in this conversation of the heart. To withhold parts of life from that conversation is, in fact, to withhold part of life from the sovereignty of God. Thus these psalms make the important connection: Everything must be *brought to speech*, and everything brought to speech must be *addressed to God*, who is the final reference for all of life."[11]

I said earlier that I was surprised that when Israel recorded its faith it didn't deny or banish the darkness from its religious experience. But what is more remarkable is that as I studied these psalms of disorientation, I found that *never one time does the psalmist say he no longer trusts in God*. Even in the darkest of the psalms God is perceived as one who is present in and attentive to the disorientations of life. And it is this kind of stubborn, protesting and lamenting faith that brings new life in deathly places.

But now I want to speak of another kind of darkness.

The cry of man's anguish went up unto God,
    "Lord, take away pain!
The shadow that darkens the world Thou hast made;
    The close-coiling chain
That strangles the heart; the burden that weighs
    On wings that would soar—
Lord, take away pain from the world Thou hast made,
    That it love Thee the more!"

Then answered the Lord to the cry of His world:
    "Shall I take away pain,
And with it the power of the soul to endure,
    Made strong by the strain?
Shall I take away pity, that knits heart to heart,
    And sacrifice high?
Will ye lose all your heroes that lift from the fire
    White brows to the sky?
Shall I take away love, that redeems with a price,
    And smiles at its loss?
Can ye spare from your lives that would climb unto mine
    The Christ on His cross?"
                    Anonymous

CHAPTER

16

DARKNESS VISIBLE

Midway upon the journey of our life I found myself in a dark wood, where the right path was lost. Ah! how hard a thing it is to tell what this wild and rough and difficult wood was, which in thought renews my fear! So bitter is it that death is little more. But in order to treat of the good that I found in it, I will tell of the other things that I saw there.

—Dante

"Anybody who goes to a psychiatrist is crazy."

I remembered how many times I had heard that line and had always laughed. I remembered it as I stared at the words on the door I was about to open: Doctor of Psychiatry. It had taken me ten years to get to this door.

Everyone said we handled the suicide of our son admirably, an inspiring Christian example of faith. And I thought we had. Surrounded by family and Christian friends, tasting the sufficiency of God's grace and overwhelmed by peace that passes understanding, we made it through those horrible days. A beautiful example of what the victorious Christian life is all about, one close friend wrote in a letter.

Ironically, at the time of Ronnie, Jr.'s illness and death, we were enjoying our greatest ministry. In the spring of 1970, God swept into our home and into our church in what could only be called a spiritual awakening. Things were happening that could only be explained by the supernatural. A seven-day-a-week, twenty-four-hour-a-day prayer ministry was launched. Repentance and restoration were almost a daily occurrence. Our worship services were characterized by an overwhelming aware-ness of God's presence. We learned about spiritual war-fare. "Praise the Lord" became the motto of our church. We honestly believed we could pray and praise our way out of anything.

But being newcomers to tragedy, we assumed the worst was behind us. The most terrible thing that could happen to parents had happened, and we had survived. Like the Israelites, when we saw the drowned Egyptians wash up on the shore of the Red Sea, we thought our enemies were destroyed.

This was during the early 70's—before the deluge of how-to books, Christian counselors, and family seminars. In Christian circles, at least in mine, no one talked about depression or death or the grieving process. No one told us that regardless of how well we were handling things now, we had been traumatized by an immense tragedy. There was no one to guide Kaye and me and the children through the grief process. If there had been, perhaps we could have escaped the things that followed. But I thought I was dealing with spiritual issues only.

DEPRESSION—THE DARK ABYSS

Early in 1976, a sense of foreboding and malaise began to settle on me. A quiet desperation took hold of my mind.

As the reality of Ronnie, Jr.'s death (no, not just death, suicide) sunk in, I decided that I had outlived my happy days. The best was past. No matter how good things might be in the future, they could never be as good as they were in the past.

I first knew I was in serious trouble while sitting on the front pew of a church one evening, waiting for the service to start. Fear suddenly gripped me—an undefined, but real, fear. I knew I could not preach that night. Walking up to the pulpit and preaching a sermon was impossible; I knew I couldn't get through it. But I had to. There was still about ten minutes before the service started, so I left the sanctuary and walked back and forth in a darkened hallway, pleading with God to get me through the service.

And He did. But there were more nights like that. I began to imagine that congregations could tell something was wrong, that they could sense my fear and see me trembling. And so I avoided people, leaving the services as soon as possible. As a matter of fact, I avoided everybody I could. I guess it was during this time that I got the reputation of being a loner. One pastor, in introducing me to his Sunday morning congregation (a large one—and on television), said, "Ron Dunn is a hard person to get to know."

A few years later, one of the things that signaled my improvement was my desire to be with people.

It was about this time that I started having the physical problems that I mentioned in chapter 4. This exacerbated the depression (which I had not yet identified or admitted to).

You need to realize that to a Christian, especially a preacher, and a victorious-life preacher at that, brought up in the fundamental Bible-belt Christianity of the South, depression was something you didn't have. And psychiatrists and psychologists were doctors you didn't go to. There was no such thing as a Christian psychologist (still isn't, according to some). After all, you've got the Bible; what more do you need? And as long as we keep separating the body from the mind, we'll go on thinking like that.

"Depression is a disorder of mood, so mysteriously painful and elusive in the way it becomes known to the self—to the mediating intellect—as to verge close to being beyond description. It thus remains nearly incomprehensible to those who have not experienced it in its extreme mode."[1]

The psychiatric literature on depression is extensive, with theory after theory about its origins. "Depression has many faces" is a statement that in some form I encountered in nearly every book I read on the subject. Doctors and clinicians vary in their opinions of what causes depression. Dr. Grace Ketterman lists a group of influences she believes intermingle to create the complex entity of depression.[2]

1. Genetic predisposition
2. Family practices and beliefs
3. Impact of the environment
4. Stress

Depression can be just as serious as any medical problem, such as diabetes or cancer. Ronnie, as a manic-depressive person, had no more control over his death than a terminal cancer patient. To say to a person suffering that kind of depression that all he needs is the Bible is like saying to a surgeon that all he needs to remove a tumor is the Bible.

Don't misunderstand me. I believe that in dealing with many problems, like some forms of depression, anger, bitterness, or marriage and family crises, all you need is the Bible. Rather, all you need is Christ and His Spirit moving through the power of the Word of God.

But I am speaking of something that goes beyond that. I had tried to handle my depression with every spiritual weapon at my disposal. In his book *The Masks of Melancholy*, Dr. John White observes:

> Unfortunately, Christians tend to see their depressions only in spiritual terms. They feel they have let God down. Religious Jews do the same, interpreting their experiences from within a religious framework. And spiritual counselors, caught up in the same thought frame, may rightly diagnose a spiritual problem in one client but miss a depressive illness in another so that faith is encouraged when faith is impossible, or praise encouraged from a heart as withered as a prune.[3]

When that happens, the symptoms are treated while the illness is allowed to progress.

TAKING A RISK?

This past June I spoke at the annual Rapha luncheon, held each year in conjunction with the annual meeting of the Southern Baptist Convention. Rapha is a nationally recognized health care organization that gives Christ-centered help for adults and adolescents suffering with psychiatric and substance abuse problems.[4]

The luncheon is primarily for pastors and their wives and addresses itself to their needs. There were about 1,300 present when I shared with them what I'm sharing with you in this chapter. A week after the luncheon I received a letter from a pastor thanking me for having the courage to risk my reputation by being transparent.

Courage? Reputation? Risk? Is that what I had done—risked my reputation by admitting that from 1976 to 1986 I fought a terrible battle with depression and had gone to a psychiatrist? That was not a pleasant thought, especially in light of the fact that more than 6,000 tapes of the luncheon have been mailed to pastors across the country.

To be honest, I have struggled with the decision to include this in the book. I know that no matter what I say or how carefully I say it, someone will misunderstand. It will be repugnant to some. Some will object to the telling of such things. Some will deny the reality of it and dismiss it as sin or lack of faith, thus trivializing the whole experience. It's a risk.

I also agree with Christian Beker that "personal experiences have a way of intruding themselves into the freedom of readers to ponder their own thoughts."[5]

I make this private matter public for one reason: I cannot forget the horror of depression—the intolerable pain, the loneliness, the hopelessness, the isolation, the despair beyond despair, "a veritable howling tempest in the brain."[6]

And I am not an exception. I want the others to know that I have been there and that there is help. For it was during this time that I discovered a serious gap in the ministry of the Church. There was no place for the "wintry" Christian. I couldn't find help in Christian books (there may have been some out there, but if so I missed them) or seminars or conferences. Sermons did not address the subject.

The truth is that I found more understanding from the world than I did from the Church; I was not afraid to speak of my feelings to the world—I was afraid where the Church was concerned. Much of this has changed now.

Meanwhile, my depression dug in (I call it depression, although at the time I still didn't know what was wrong). I began to withdraw more and more, neglecting family and ministry obligations. It is an anguish to know that for those years, when my children were growing up, I was not there for them.

I was not there, period. I had relocated, living in my own benighted world. The knowledge that genetics played a part in depression caused me to wonder whether I was to blame for Ronnie's illness and whether I would come to the same end as he had, an end, I admit, that became increasingly appealing. Oblivion was the only escape from the pain.

Novelist William Styron describes his experience in these words: "What I had begun to discover is that, mysteriously and in ways that are totally remote from normal experience, the gray drizzle of horror induced by depression takes on the quality of physical pain. But it is not an immediately identifiable pain, like that of a broken limb. It may be more accurate to say that despair, owing to some evil trick played upon the sick brain by the inhabiting psyche, comes to resemble the diabolical discomfort of being imprisoned in a fiercely overheated room. And because no breeze stirs this caldron, because there is no escape from this smothering confinement, it is entirely natural that the victim begins to think ceaselessly of oblivion."[7]

Oblivion. How sweet the thought—to escape somewhere, anywhere, beyond the reach of my relentless tormentor. But I don't think I ever seriously considered ending my life; I had witnessed in myself and in my family the devastation suicide had wrought, resulting in alternating emotions of grief and anger when I considered Ronnie's act.

Things began happening fast. Frightful things. Like memory loss. I would read a book and not remember even that I had read it, much less what I had read. People reminded me of phone conversations I knew nothing about. In Houston, I woke up one morning in my motel room to discover an extra room key and a *Wall Street Journal* that had not been there the night before. The clerk told me that I had come to the lobby about 3:00 A.M. looking for a newspaper, and the *Journal* was the only one I could find, and that I had left my key in the room. I would start a sentence, only to stop midway, unable to think of words.

Such memory lapses chipped away at my self-confidence until I no longer trusted my own judgment. I became more and more dependent upon Kaye. Her most vivid picture of this time is of me shuffling about the house like a feeble old man, head bowed and shoulders hunched. Panic or anxiety attacks became a frequent occurrence, times when I would seethe with rage, a revved-up sensation that I could feel in my teeth and gums and fingertips. I often found myself standing in the middle of a room, paralyzed, staring at nothing.

It was Kaye who first suspected that I was suffering from depression. I remember the morning well. We were in Little Rock, and I was to begin a meeting that Sunday morning. But I couldn't get out of bed—I just lay there and cried, as I had done many times when she was not present. The thought of getting up, showering, shaving, brushing my teeth, combing my hair, choosing a shirt, buttoning it, selecting a tie, tying it, putting on my shoes, going out to the car—well, you get the picture.

Remarkably, that Sunday morning a young man approached me after the service and said, "I hear you are having stomach problems. I believe I can help you." He was a doctor specializing in stomach disorders. I visited him the next morning, and he asked me a hundred questions. For the first time I began to open up. That was the beginning of my recovery; the stomach problems were soon under control.

But the depression persisted, and I finally admitted I needed "more" help. I called Kaye from Tulsa one day and told her I couldn't take it anymore. She had to find a—psychiatrist. And she did. A close friend recommended a fine Christian doctor. I opened the door and went in.

In my reading and research I fish from many ponds, as you may have noticed, perhaps with some concern. Truth is where you find it. That doesn't mean I keep every fish I pull from a pond. Many I throw back. But this one is a keeper. I pulled it from Thomas Moore's pond, *The Care of the Soul.* In a chapter entitled "Gifts of Depression," Moore writes:

> The soul presents itself in a variety of colors, including all the shades of gray, blue and black. To care for the soul, we must observe the full range of all its colorings, and resist the temptation to approve only of white, red, and orange— the brilliant colors. The "bright" idea of colorizing old black and white movies is consistent with our culture's general rejection of the dark and the gray. In a society that is defended against the tragic sense of life, depression will appear as an enemy, an unredeemable malady; yet in such a society, devoted to light, depression, in compensation, will be unusually strong. . . . We may have to develop a taste for the depressed mood, a positive respect for its place in the soul's cycles. . . .
>
> Melancholy gives the soul an opportunity to express a side of its nature that is as valid as any other, but is hidden out of our distaste for darkness and bitterness."[8]

Remember the man born blind we discussed in chapter 11? I said that a whole man would have been of little use to Jesus that day. To display the works of God he needed someone with an unanswered "why" in his life.

About three years ago I was weed-eating my dad's lawn. I don't know how it is with you, but some of my greatest revelations come, not when I'm in the prayer closet, but when I'm doing something as mundane as weed-eating. Anyway, I was reflecting on the past few years of my ministry, and it occurred to me that one word had come to characterize it. It was not my word, but the word of those who came to hear me preach: *encouragement.* I hadn't made the connection before, but lately pastorless churches had called me to say they were hurting and needed to be encouraged. Could I come?

I didn't set out to become a preacher of encouragement. It just sort of happened. But the remarkable thought I had while I chewed up my dad's weeds was that all those sermons that were encouraging people were prepared and preached during the darkest days of my life. Go figure.

My Leader and I . . . mounted up, he first and I second, so far that through a round opening I saw some of the beautiful things which Heaven bears, and thence we issued forth again to see the stars.

—Dante

146

CHAPTER
17

WHEN THE LIGHTS GO OUT

Some darkness is self-inflicted.

In the early years of our marriage, when the children were small, our idea of a fun vacation was checking into a motel for a few days, playing in the swimming pool, and eating in the restaurant. Strange as it sounds now, that was an exciting event. It didn't take a great deal to excite us.

One summer we spent a few days visiting Kaye's parents in Little Rock, Arkansas, then drove to Hot Springs and checked into a motel. Hot Springs offers a lot to see and do for tourists, but I don't think we left the motel swimming pool long enough to do any sight-seeing. Who wanted to drive around looking at things when you could be doing belly-busters in a neat pool?

I left early to fulfill a preaching assignment back in Dallas, arriving home around midnight. It was a smoldering August night. I unlocked the door and switched on the lights. No light; the ceiling bulb must be burned out. Boy, it's hot in here, I thought. Better have the freon checked in the air-conditioner. I stumbled around in the darkness and found a lamp and switched it on. No light. I switched and switched. No light. By the time I had tried three or four more switches, I unwillingly admitted to myself that the electricity had been shut off. No wonder it's so hot in here. I located a candle and some matches and found the notice on the front door, informing me that our electricity had been shut off for nonpayment of our bill. It wasn't that we didn't have the money; in those days I handled the money and the bills and occasionally in my disorganized oblivion, I forgot some things. (For obvious reasons, Kaye now handles those matters.)

It was then that I remembered the deer meat in the freezer. A few days before we left on vacation a church-member, cleaning out his deepfreeze, thought we might like some venison, and brought over several pounds, which we had not yet touched.

I won't attempt to describe the smell that leaped out at me when I opened the freezer door. What can I say? It was rotten deer meat—generously covered with a gallon of melted chocolate ice cream that had been sitting on the top shelf.

That night candlelight forever lost its romantic ambience for me. I spent several hours in its flickering flame scraping chocolate-covered deer meat, not to mention assorted vegetables, from the freezer.

And the worst part was that I couldn't blame anybody but myself.

I think you see what I'm getting at. Sometimes the lights go out because of our neglect of spiritual obligations or just plain old disobedience. You already know what to do about that.

But for the kind of darkness Isaiah is describing, he gives some definite instructions.

KEEP ON WALKING

During a question-and-answer period at a conference, a woman asked, "What do you do when you don't know what to do?"

We had been discussing guidance and knowing the will of God. I thought for a moment then said, "Do what you know to do."

When you don't know what to do, do what you know to do. Or in Isaiah's words, keep walking.

When the lights go out, our immediate reaction is to stop dead still. In some situations, that's the right thing to do. During an all-night drive back home after a week-long meeting, my car lights suddenly went out. I didn't have to pray about what to do; I pulled off on the shoulder and waited until daylight. That was the right thing to do.

But not in the spiritual realm. Isaiah says that those who fear the Lord and obey His commands are those who keep walking when darkness descends. The Hebrew construction seems to say that this is the characteristic of the trusting servant.

One of the men in the hotel room (chapter 16) testified that although he was living in darkness, he continued his personal worship time with prayer and Bible study.

What are we to do when our prayers stick in our throat, when it seems that God has stuffed cotton in His ears, when we are praying in cold blood? Keep praying. During one of the rougher periods of my depression, when it seemed as though I would never get better, Kaye, who had prayed faithfully from the first, became discouraged. "I keep praying, but it doesn't seem to do any good."

"Don't stop praying!" I said. "I'll get through this. Your prayers will be answered."

And they were.

C. S. Lewis faced this same sense of despair concerning prayer during the terminal illness of his wife: "What chokes every prayer and every hope is the memory of all the prayers H. and I offered and all the false hopes we had. Not hopes raised merely by our own wishful thinking; hopes encouraged, even forced upon us, by false diagnoses, by X-ray photographs, by strange remissions, by one temporary recovery that might have ranked as a miracle."[1]

Keep walking. Keep praying, reading the Bible, witnessing to others, going to church, singing the hymns—when you don't know what to do, do what you know to do.

DON'T LIGHT YOUR OWN FIRE

Listen again to the words of the prophet. After telling us to trust the Lord in the dark, he says:

> "But instead, some of you want to light
> your own fires and make your own light.
> So, go, walk in the light of your fires,
> and trust your own light to guide you.
> But this is what you will receive from me:
> You will lie down in a place of pain." (v. 11, NCV)

Man-made light is dangerous and deceptive. When I was a pastor, weddings were my least favorite thing to do. So much can go wrong. About one hour before a Saturday afternoon wedding, I put on my rented tux. I had been measured for it a few days before at the rental shop. But in the meantime, someone fouled up. The trousers (when you're talking about a tuxedo, it's trousers, not pants) fit perfectly, but the coat swallowed me alive. There was enough room for me and the groom both in there. I did what anybody would do; I panicked and ran down to the store and got another coat. I tried it on in the store, and it fit perfectly. But when I walked into the sunlight, I discovered that black comes in different shades—and I was wearing two of them. But it didn't matter; the wedding would be in the sanctuary under man-made light, and no one would notice the error.

How many times have you taken your socks to the window to see if they were black or blue? Man-made light is deceptive and can be dangerous.

Abraham found that out when, during the darkness of Sarah's barrenness, he lit his own fire with Hagar. And Moses found out by killing the Egyptian. (Did he think he could deliver Israel by killing one Egyptian at a time?) And Israel, at Kadesh-barnea, lit their own fire by sending out the spies to see if they could do what God had already told them to do. And then there was Peter, drawing his sword in the garden.

What is so dangerous about the dark is that we often get so desperate to *see* something happen, we take it upon ourselves to see that it does. An infamous proverb says, "A miracle is a miracle, even if the Devil did it"—concerned only with the deed, not the agent.[2]

I remember a series of meetings I held in a church in Oklahoma. It was the deadest church I had ever been in. It was so dead, you had to say it in two syllables—da-uhd. On the last night, the music director, only ten minutes into the service (usually the song service is about thirty minutes long), turned to me and said, "It's yours," and went over and sat down. During that brief song service I noticed in the congregation an elderly woman I had not seen before. I noticed her because during one of the hymns she raised her hands. Leaning over to the pastor, I whispered, "She must be a visitor." He nodded and said, "She is."

Well, I struggled through my sermon and gave an invitation (it was a revival-type meeting, and each service ended with an appeal for people to come forward to receive Christ or join the church, and so forth).

No one came forward—except the hand-raising visitor. She spoke to the pastor, and he came to the microphone and told the congregation the woman had something to say. He made a mistake by not asking her what she wanted to say.

Well, she came to the microphone and read some obscure verse from Ezekiel, spat out a few scathing words of exhortation, and extended an invitation. The choir sang another verse. No one responded. She turned to Isaiah and read another obscure verse and said a few more words. But this time she came down hard on the women in the congregation, admonishing them to come to the altar and pray. The congregation was paralyzed by shock. One or two brave women came and knelt at the altar.

Suddenly the music director was at my side and said, "Do you think this is of God?"

I said, "I don't know, but it's something!"

The darkness is ordained of God. Oswald Chambers said that God sometimes withdraws His conscious blessings to teach us to trust Him more perfectly.[3] In the opening words of his Gospel, John declares, "The Light shines in the darkness, and the darkness has not overpowered it" (John 1:5, NCV).

Do you know what darkness is? It is the absence of light. Profound, eh? If you're sitting in a lighted room at night and open the door, does darkness flood the room? No. Darkness cannot chase away the light. Darkness can only enter the room when the light has been removed. The night does not force the day to leave; the day leaves and night follows.

The Genesis creation account tells us that "evening and morning were the first day." Did you know that evening is just as much a part of the day as morning? Night is a part of the twenty-four-hour day. We say there are twenty-four hours in a day, not twenty-four hours in a night.

If there is darkness, it is because God, for reasons known only to Him, has withdrawn the light. Making our own light frustrates the purpose of God.

There are some things you can see only in the dark. When you live in a big city as I do, it's hard to see the stars at night. One of the things I enjoyed most about the nights we used to spend on our farm in the country was how brightly the stars shone in the sky. Somewhere I read these words of Annie Dillard: "You do not have to sit outside in the dark. If, however, you want to look at the stars, you will find that darkness is required. The stars neither require it or demand it."[4]

LEAN ON ME

Isaiah says that the one walking in darkness is to "rely on his God." The King James Version reads, "stay upon his God." The word means to lean for support. In Psalm 23, the root of that word is translated "staff": "Thy rod and Thy staff comfort me." "Support me" is the meaning of the word *comfort*. It reminds me of the words of Proverbs, "Trust in the LORD with all your heart and *lean not on your own understanding*" (Prov. 3:5, italics added).

When God withdraws the light, He is trying to teach us that there is something better than light—faith. As the words of the old hymn say:

> When the light of your life grows dim,
> Still cling to Jesus, sink or swim.
> Still at His throne bow the knee,
> And Israel's God thy strength shall be.

153

Part Four: What to Remember When You Can't Forget
The Ministry of Disappointment

"Whatever men expect, they soon come to think they have a right to; the sense of disappointment can, with very little skill on our part, be turned into a sense of injury."

Screwtape to Wormwood
The Screwtape Letters, C. S. Lewis

"a whisper
Which Memory will warehouse as a shout."

Owen Barfield

One day it will be realized that men are as distinguished from one another as much by the forms their memories take as by their character.

André Malraux

18

MEMORY: MINISTER OR MONSTER?

One evening back in 1984, as I was dressing for church, I flipped on the network news. The reporter was talking about a new board game that was sweeping the country. Not since Monopoly had a board game taken the nation with such a storm. Store owners were unable to keep it in stock; as soon as it appeared on the shelves, it disappeared. At twenty-seven dollars a piece, that amounted to a lot of money. Always on the cutting edge of "what's happening," I had never heard of it.

It was a genuine phenomenon, the reporter said. And then he interviewed one of the three inventors of the game. Asked how they came to invent the game, the man told how the three of them had been together one evening and decided to play Scrabble. But they couldn't find the Scrabble board. So they set out to make up their own game, and forty-five minutes later, there was Trivial Pursuit.

The reporter asked his guest, "How do you explain the overwhelming response to your game? Why are people buying it?"

I wasn't prepared for the philosophical answer the man gave. "Oh," he said, "they're just buying memories. That's all you can buy with your money—memories."

My immediate thought was: "I have some memories I would like to sell! As a matter of fact, I have some memories I'll give away. As a matter of fact, I have some memories I will *pay* you to take off my mind."

Don't you?

Memory—can't live without it, and some can't live with it; so they seek asylum in drugs or drink or death. Memory can be a minister one minute and a monster the next. We have memories we run to and memories we run from; we hide from them in a closet of busyness, trying to block them out, to head them off at the pass. But eventually they overtake us. At some unguarded moment, they pounce on us, bringing with them all the disappointments of the past.

In *A Prayer for Owen Meany*, John Irving says, "Your memory is a monster; *you* forget—it doesn't. It simply files things away. It keeps things for you, or hides things from you—and summons them to a recall with a will of its own. You think you have a memory; but it has you!"[1]

Memory is the video camera of the mind; it records everything, forgets nothing. You may think it has forgotten, but something, a word, an insignificant incident, a song, a smell—anything can trigger the memory, and suddenly it's dragging barbed-wire through your stomach.

DOWN MEMORY LANE

My mind is in league with my memory, and sometimes my mind will start leading me down a path of the past. I know where that particular path ends up; it ends up in the cemetery of disappointments, and once there, memory will resurrect every dead dream, every heartache, every betrayal. Memory has no mercy. So when my mind starts heading in that direction, I make a deliberate decision to turn it in another direction: to the place of praise and thanksgiving. Sometimes I make it, and sometimes I don't.

I think about the rich man in hell and hear his pitiful cry for just a drop of water on his tongue. "Send Lazarus," he begs. But Abraham replies, "Son, *remember* that in your lifetime you received your good things, while Lazarus received bad things, but now he is comforted here and you are in agony" (Luke 16:25, emphasis added). *Remember.* The man's memory was more painful than any fire in hell.

Memory is capricious; it is exceedingly selective. Through the years many people have done a lot of nice things for me; I don't remember all of them. But I've not forgotten one who treated me unkindly. Through the years people have said a lot of nice things about my sermons. I don't remember many of them. But I've never forgotten a single person who criticized my preaching. If you want to make a lasting impression on me, tell me this book stinks. I promise I will never forgive, uh, forget you.

HEALING MEMORIES

We hear a lot today about the healing of memories. Back in the seventies, President Jimmy Carter's sister, Ruth Carter Stapleton, popularized this idea in her two books describing how the process works. The healing of memories "begins with the assumption that many present problems arise from traumatic 'dark and painful memories' that are buried in 'the deep mind, that region which carefully records and stores every experience of life.' "[2] Then as now, Christian leaders and counselors were deeply divided over the legitimacy of this "ministry."

But I think there can be no doubt that many of the present maladjustments in our lives are the residue of deep, dark, and dismal disappointments and the result of not having made peace with these unforgettable wounds. The past casts its shadow over the present.

Disappointment in unanswered prayer makes us suspicious of all praying. Disillusioned by a trusted minister, we may distrust all ministers. Disappointment with your children can make you wish birth control was retroactive. And then when God lets you down, that is the biggest disappointment of all. Not dealt with properly, disappointment degenerates into bitterness and that into cynicism.

Of course, the thing to do is to forget about it and get on with your life. Ah, there is no shortage of that kind of advice. That's why advice is cheap—overproduction.

"Forgive and forget" is my favorite. I've never found that in the Bible, but it doesn't seem to discourage people from offering it. As far as I know, God is the only one who has the ability to forget on demand. As a matter of fact, the best way to remember something is to try to forget it.

Some of those hurts, those lost hopes, dead dreams and failed expectations—disappointments—you will never forget. So stop trying.

I would like to suggest that rather than struggling to forget those things, you instead *remember* something else. When you can't forget, remember.

This was God's counsel to David.

You can read about it in the seventeenth chapter of 1 Chronicles. It was a time of calm for the warrior-king. For the present, God had given him victory over his enemies. There would be future battles, of course, but for now David was doing what he loved to do most: sitting in his house, meditating on the law of God. And what a house it was—a palace built of cedars. But there was something about it that didn't seem right.

So one evening, visiting with Nathan the prophet, David speaks of the matter that has been disturbing him and reveals the desire of his heart.

"It is not right," David says as he gazes about his palace, "that I should live in such luxury, while the Ark of God at this very moment is in a tent."

Immediately Nathan knew where David was going with this thought. A temple! A magnificent temple! At last, a permanent dwelling place for the Ark!

"Yes!" Nathan says. "Do all that is in your heart—God is with you!"

But later that night, when Nathan returns to his own quarters, the prophet discovers that he has spoken too quickly, for the Lord has a message waiting for him. Nathan, son, you missed that one. "Go and tell my servant David, 'This is what the Lord says: You are not the one to build me a house to dwell in'" (v. 4).

For one exhilarating moment David grasped in his hand his greatest dream—only to have it torn from him the next moment. How did David deal with the death of his dream, this overwhelming disappointment? How does anybody?

Let's take a quick peek at the end of the story and see if we can catch David's response to this bad news.

When you hear of David's terrible disappointment, you would half expect him to spend the night on his bed shedding bitter tears—and not blame him. Which only shows how little we know of this man after God's own heart.

Rather than fleeing to his room and slamming the door in self-pity and anger, he immediately humbles himself before the Lord. "Who am I, O Lord God, and what is my family, that you have brought me this far? And as if this were not enough in your sight, O God, you have spoken about the future of the house of your servant. You have looked on me as though I were the most exalted before men, O Lord God. What more can David say to you for honoring your servant?" (see vv. 16–18)

He then lifts praises to His Lord and His people: "There is no one like you, O Lord, and there is no God but you. . . . And who is like your people Israel—the one nation on earth whose God went out to redeem a people for himself, and to make a name for yourself" (see vv. 20–21).

What David did next was remarkable. Knowing that he might die before the temple's completion, and considering Solomon's youth and inexperience, David made preparations that would enable his son to fulfill the task. He became a fundraiser for the project. And he was pretty successful. "I have taken great pains," said David to his son, "to provide for the temple of the Lord a hundred thousand talents of gold, a million talents of silver, quantities of bronze and iron too great to be weighed, and wood and stone. . . . Now begin the work, and the Lord be with you" (see 22:14–16).

I would say David handled his disappointment fairly well, wouldn't you? How did he do it?

God told him to *remember*.

When we can't forget, we need to remember that . . .

19

A GOOD IDEA IS NOT NECESSARILY GOD'S IDEA

Sometimes I wish I had not written my book on prayer, *Don't Just Stand There, Pray Something.* When you write a book like that, people get the idea you know what you're talking about. But we always say more about prayer than we understand. Prayer belongs in the category of mystery; there's more about it that we don't understand than we do understand. At least that's true for me.

Anyway, I receive a lot of wonderful letters sharing the joy of answered prayer. And I get others—letters of acute disappointment because of unanswered requests. Can I please tell them what they did wrong? Occasionally, someone will write, not to ask advice, but to inform me that prayer didn't work.

I received a letter from one reader who listed twelve unanswered prayers. After each failed account, he wrote: "So much for intercession."

Reading my book had brought back the memories of those unanswered prayers—bitter disappointments that he could not forget. But he is not alone. In the book I state that God did not answer the two biggest prayers of my life: the healing of my mother and the healing of my son. Those are disappointments I will never forget.

But it's hard to be objective when you're seeking God's will about something like that. Surely, God can't think of letting them die. But our idea is not always God's idea. As I will try to show later, God's idea is always best.

I think of a couple who inherited a large sum of money and wanted to use it in a way that would honor God. They were approached by two fellow churchmembers who were ready to launch an exciting new Christian endeavor. All they needed was a little more financial backing. They got it. And they've still got it—wherever they are. Nobody knows, least of all the couple who only wanted to serve God with their money. Hurt, angry, bitter, they vowed never to return to church.

To this couple, it seemed like a good idea at the time. They even prayed about it. And for seventeen years they blamed God for their disappointment. But they came finally to acknowledge that a good idea is not always God's idea.

A SCARY ISSUE

Many believers are terrified of the phrase "discovering the will of God," which probably isn't a legitimate phrase, anyway.[1] Christians often get uptight about this issue. "Why is this?" J. I. Packer says: "The source of anxiety is that a desire for guidance is linked with uncertainty about how to get it and fear of the consequences of not getting it."[2] Feeling wholly unqualified for the task, they doubt their ability to discern the will of God for themselves.

And not only that but "our wants have an uncanny way of influencing our thoughts and our opinions."[3] Often, in seeking guidance, we are really seeking God's approval of what we want to do or have already decided to do.

If this describes you, you need to know you're in good company.

David had a good idea. Actually, it was a great idea; Nathan the prophet thought so too. Build God a temple, a dwelling place for the ark. This was not a whim. Listen to the holy zeal that burned in David's heart:

> "O LORD, remember David
>   and all the hardships he endured.
> He swore an oath to the LORD
>   and made a vow to the Mighty One of Jacob;
> 'I will not enter my house
>   or go to my bed—
> I will allow no sleep to my eyes,
>   no slumber to my eyelids,
> till I find a place for the LORD,
>   a dwelling for the Mighty One of Jacob.'"
> > (Psalm 132:1–5, NIV)

By all accounts, building a temple seemed the right thing to do. After all, the Ark *was* in a tent. And David's motives were pure. His intent was to express his gratitude to the Lord for all He had done for His servant. David wanted to crown his reign with a temple that would stand forever in Jerusalem, a breathtaking monument to the glory of God.

The truth is that we may not always know God's specific will for every detail of our lives. We may learn it only as He unfolds it step by step. Each of us builds his or her own system of discerning God's will, but God is bigger than our systems and our theology. We must develop a tolerance for ambiguity.

BATTLERS AND BUILDERS

Do you know why God would not permit David to build the temple? We're told in 1 Chronicles 22:8: "But this word of the LORD came to me: 'You have shed much blood and have fought many wars. You are not to build a house for my Name, because you have shed much blood on the earth in my sight.'"

David had bloody hands, and bloody hands could not build the sacred house of the Lord. Now, this wasn't a condemnation of David. He had shed blood because he was a warrior-king. That was his task in the Kingdom of God. David was a battler, not a builder.

The next verse says, "But you will have a son who will be a man of peace and rest, and I will give him rest from all his enemies on every side. His name will be Solomon, and I will grant Israel peace and quiet during his reign. He is the one who will build a house for my Name."

David was a battler; Solomon was a builder. And so it is that God Himself sets us to our tasks. Some are called to battle; others are called to build.

Understand this: David's failure was not God's failure. The temple was built.

My happiest days as a pastor were at my last church. The fellowship was harmonious and sweet, and we experienced incredible growth. Of course, I received much of the credit because of my "outstanding" leadership! Actually the church was in a booming area, and we would have had to lock the doors to keep from growing. But that was not the real secret.

What people did not know was that the church had a history of trouble. There was a small group of men who pretty much "ran" the church—they ran one pastor off and were instrumental in causing another to leave. But when my predecessor arrived, whom I knew very well, things changed. I always thought of him as a bantam rooster, always ready for a fight. Well, he called the god squad together and said, "This church isn't big enough for all of us, and I'm not leaving."

And he didn't. He grabbed hold of the horns of that bull and rode it for the count. Eventually, those men moved on, and the foundation was laid for a great church. That pastor never saw his vision fulfilled. But I did.

Now the point is, I am not a battler. I'm not good at confrontation; I don't think I could have done what he did. He was the battler, I was the builder. Unfortunately, it's usually the builder who gets all the credit. But he doesn't deserve it.

You may have a great idea, but it may not be God's idea.

You may have a great idea, but it may not be God's idea for you *at this time.*

You may have a great idea, and it may be God's idea, *but not for you.*

A FORGOTTEN MAN'S VISION

From 1903 until 1989, a grand, historic church graced downtown Memphis, Tennessee. Made famous by the oratorical splendor of its Bible-preaching pastor, Dr. Robert G. Lee, who served from 1927 to 1960, the Bellevue Baptist Church became, and remains, one of the most prestigious pulpits in the country.

But the church was landlocked; there was no room to grow. Adjoining downtown property was too expensive, so under the leadership of its present pastor, Dr. Adrian Rogers, plans were formulated to relocate this historic church. Now, unless you have ever attempted such a mammoth, emotion-charged project, you have no idea of the problems involved.

But property was found seventeen miles out on the edge of Memphis in Cordova, Tennessee. Purchasing land from five different owners, the church acquired four hundred acres. But it was practically inaccessible, with only one small road leading to it. Nearly two million dollars were spent on roads leading to and from the property.

And in 1989, the Bellevue Baptist Church took possession of one of the most beautiful and spacious church plants in the country. The worship center seats 7,000 people to accommodate the crowds they have at two Sunday morning services. There are 31 acres of asphalt parking, 8 miles of curb, 1,285 doors, 65 water fountains, over 200 staff members, 50 restrooms, 87 public telephones, and over 22,000 members. The building cost 34 million dollars and has an annual budget of 8 million dollars.

But the most important facts of the church aren't physical and material; they are spiritual. It is one of the most vibrant and alive churches I have ever seen; it is a great church, not because of its physical assets, but because of the blessings of God upon its people.

But there is one more important part of the story. One of the five men who sold his property to the church told the buyers: "You know where I got my piece of property? I bought it from an old Baptist preacher who used to walk over that plot of ground, praying that someday God would build a Baptist church there."

The old preacher had a great vision, a vision he failed to see fulfilled. But his failure was not God's failure. The temple was built.

20

GOD JUDGES US, NOT BY THE ACHIEVEMENTS OF OUR HANDS, BUT BY THE AMBITION OF OUR HEART

Because it was in your heart to build a Temple for my Name,
you did well to have this in your heart. (2 Chron. 6:8)

God is the only master I know who pays his servants as much for the ambition in their hearts as for the actions of their hands.

One night in the earlier stages of our son's difficulties, before we understood he was manic-depressive, I found Kaye sitting at the kitchen table with her face in her hands, crying.

I put my arm around her and asked, "Honey, what's wrong?"

"I feel like such a failure as a mother," she said.

She wasn't the first mother to say that, and certainly not the last. But I strongly disagreed with her. "Honey," I said, "You're the best mother I know. You love your kids, you spend time with them—you are not a failure!"

And then I had a crazy thought: Hey, maybe it's the children who are the failures. Maybe we're great parents with bad kids!

I'm just joking, of course (?), but don't you sometimes feel there is a grand conspiracy to make parents feel guilty? You know what I mean. I was always taught that it was imperative to spend time with my children—and I did. Then someone came along and said, "It's not just time, it's got to be *quality* time." What on earth is *quality time!*

Visit your bookstores, Christian and secular; they will have a section on parenting—a big section. Have you ever seen so much material in books, on tapes and TV, and in seminars on parenting? Yet we see very little improvement in the home life of our nation, even among Christians. Many of the Christian parents I talk with are haunted by fears of failure, just plain scared to death they're not going to measure up. They've been told that

> Good parents rear good children.
> Bad parents rear bad children.

BUT IT'S NOT THAT SIMPLE

While writing this chapter, Kaye and I had lunch with a couple of friends at a local restaurant not far from the church I pastored for nine years. I guess because I was writing on this section at the time, I remembered something about the place. On our way out, I glanced at a large booth in the corner; it was the booth our staff occupied many times during lunch break on staff-meeting days. I was young, fat, and sassy in those days, with three small children, and I recalled sitting there with my staff discussing the teenage son of one of our couples in the church. It was in the late sixties when rebellion, long hair, and drugs were the rage among young people and the scourge among parents.

I remember sitting there shaking my head and, God forgive me, saying, "Well, there must be something wrong in that home if he's acting that way." The parents appeared to be fine Christians when they were at church, but obviously they weren't fine Christians when they were home.

As we left the restaurant, I could see the street corner where a few years later my own son, in rebellion and long hair during one of his manic-depressive episodes, stood selling roses on Sunday while most of my churchmembers drove by on their way to hear me preach.

The other day, Kaye related a conversation she had with our twenty-eight-year-old daughter. They were talking along these same lines. Kim said, "Mom, you and Dad were great parents. We just did some stupid things." Well, doing stupid things is not the sole province of children. Parents live in the same neighborhood.

But that's the trouble with being a parent; by the time you're experienced, you're unemployed.

The truth is, as John White says, "we can neither take all the credit for our children when they turn out well nor all the blame when they turn out badly. Genes, home environment, school and social environment, and the child's capacities to make certain choices all bear on the final outcome."[1]

Whatever the outcome, I want to be able to say, "Dear Lord, I made many mistakes, but you know it was in my heart to be the best father I could be."

THE OLD PERFORMANCE TRAP

After an evening service, a distraught young woman sought me out. "I must talk to you about my quiet time." Before I had a chance to reply, she plunged on.

"I know we're supposed to spend an hour or so in the morning with the Lord in prayer and Bible study before we go to work or wherever. But I have to get up at 5:30 A.M. to get myself ready for work and the kids for school and my husband for work and fix breakfast and lunches for the kids. I've tried getting up an hour earlier, at 4:30, because I know that's what I'm supposed to do, but I just can't do it! What do I do?"

"Don't worry about it," I said.

She was momentarily stunned speechless by this flagrant irreverence, so I plunged on. "In the first place, the Bible nowhere commands us to spend an hour or even a minute in prayer before we leave our house in the morning. It does say a lot about rising early in the morning, and a lot of spiritual writers through the years have championed the idea. But the Bible does not command us to do it at a specific hour or for a specific length of time.

"Pick a time that suits your schedule, a time when you're comfortable and alert. My own time is midnight. It doesn't have to be a test of physical endurance to be spiritual."

We continue to perpetuate an American myth that sounds wonderful and is well-intended, but can be painfully damaging: "You can be anything you want to be!"

But you can't be anything you want to be, not that we shouldn't try. But there are limits, set by nature, by God, by the real world.

One writer says that sometimes to become whole, we have to give up the Dream. "The Dream is the vision we had when we were young—perhaps planted by our parents or teachers, perhaps flowering from within our own imaginations—that we would be somebody truly special. We dreamed that our names would be famous, that our work would be recognized, that our marriages would be perfect and our children exemplary. When things do not turn out that way, we feel like failures. We will never be happy until we stop measuring our real-life achievements against that Dream."[2]

Of course, this doesn't mean we aren't to seek to achieve. As we saw earlier, David threw himself into the task of raising the necessary means to build the temple—and his achievement was great. The ambition of your heart will direct the aim of your hands.

Remember the old Baptist preacher we talked about in the last chapter, the one who walked over his parcel of ground, praying that one day God would build a church there? Well, I have a feeling he will share as much in the reward of that great work as if he had built it himself.

You may never be as good a parent as you desire, but if it is in your heart, do your best and trust God with the rest.

You may never accomplish great things for God, as the world counts greatness, but is it in your heart?

You may never become the preacher you long to be, but is it in your heart?

You may never see your church grow into a large congregation, but is it in your heart?

You may never win that friend to Christ, but is it in your heart?

You may never see your children serve God as you wish them to, but is it in your heart?

You did well to have this in your heart.

CHAPTER
21

WHEN GOD SAYS NO, IT IS NOT TO DEPRIVE US OF A BLESSING, BUT TO DRIVE US TO A BETTER ONE

David had a great idea.

God had a better one.

David's great idea was to build a house for God.

God's better idea was to build a house for David.

When Nathan returned to David's house to deliver God's message, he said, "King, I have some bad news and some good news. The bad news is that you can't build a house for the Lord. But the good news is, the Lord will build a house for you" (see 1 Chron. 17:10).

When David heard that he went in and sat before the Lord and said:

"Who am I, O LORD God, and what is my family, that you have brought me this far? And as if this were not enough

175

in your sight, O God, you have spoken about the future of the house of your servant. . . .

"And now, LORD, let the promise you have made concerning your servant and his house be established forever. Do as you promised, so that it will be established and that your name will be great forever. . . . And the house of your servant David will be established before you.

"You, my God, have revealed to your servant that you will build a house for him. So your servant has found courage to pray to you. O LORD, you are God! You have given this good promise to your servant. Now you have been pleased to bless the house of your servant, that it may continue forever in your sight; for you, O LORD, have blessed it, and it will be blessed forever."

(1 Chron. 17:16, 23–27, NIV)

Did you notice how many times the word *forever* was used? When God builds a house for his servant, it lasts forever. But when we try to build something for God it—well, it doesn't last quite that long.

David thought that the best thing he could do to honor God was to build a magnificent temple that would stand forever. The Temple was finally built by David's son Solomon, and it lasted until 589 B.C. when it was destroyed by Nebuchadnezzar. The Second Temple, Zerrubabel's Temple, stood from 527 to 168 B.C. The final temple, Herod's Temple, was built in A.D. 19 and was destroyed by the Romans in A.D. 70. Today, the Muslim shrine called the "Dome of the Rock," or the Mosque of Omar, stands on the Temple site. So much for man's everlasting memorials to God.

But David did leave something behind, called the Psalms, I believe. And not a jot or tittle of that has passed away. And, of course, the Seed of David. And the House of David.

THE GREATER BLESSING—REMEMBRANCE

When God sent Nathan back to David with the bad news that he wouldn't be permitted to build the temple, God sent along another word. It's as though God was saying, "I know David, and when he hears this news, he's going to puff up and pout. He'll roll into a little ball of self-pity and feel sorry for himself. So before he has a chance to do that, tell him this also."

So God said to Nathan, "Now then, tell my servant David, 'This is what the Lord Almighty says: I took you from the pasture and from following the flock, to be ruler over my people Israel. I have been with you wherever you have gone, and I have cut off all your enemies from before you. Now I will make your name like the names of the greatest men of the earth.'"

Do you see what God is doing? He is reminding David of where he was when God found him. In the pasture. Following the flock (which being interpreted is, watch your step). David, before you complain about the one thing you can't have, remember all that you do have. Before you lament over what I haven't given you, remember all that I have given to you.

A TALE OF A BALLOON

Six Flags Over Texas! That's all our kids could talk about—a giant theme park that rivaled Disneyland. And just ten miles from our house. And everybody, I mean, everybody was going. Except them, of course. Oh, Daddy, please!

I didn't want to go, couldn't afford to go. That place was expensive. But what could I do? I was supposed to spend *quality* time with my children. And quality time was time spent at Six Flags Over Texas.

And so we went. On a Saturday in August when three-fourths of the civilized world was there. It opened at 10:00 A.M. and we were there early; we had to be to find a parking place on that gargantuan parking lot, then catch a ride on a trolley to the front gate. "Honey, did you notice what our row number was?" Huh?

At the gate we paid our money, a lot for a young pastor of a young Baptist church, went through the turnstile, got our hands stamped with the mark of the beast, and we were in. Six Flags Over Texas.

The place was hot, humid, and bursting with sweating, screaming human bodies. And the lines. We had to stand in line thirty minutes for a thirty-second ride. I looked for the shortest lines, no matter where they led; but that was deceptive because the lines were serpentine, and when you rounded the corner you were staring at a thousand people in front of you.

We rode the Log Roll six times. The kids put me in the front seat because that's where all the water went when you hit the bottom.

Quality time.

And then it was 6:00 P.M., and I gathered everyone around and said, "Hey, this has been great! Right, kids? Boy, I'm glad you made me come! Well, let's go home now."

"Oh no, Dad, no! They're open till midnight. We've still got six more hours!"

By the time we got out of the park, jumped on a trolley, found our car, found the way out, and got on the highway it was 1:00 A.M. In five hours I had to be up, getting ready for the early morning worship service. I had spent over a hundred dollars! But it was quality time.

The children were asleep in the back seat; Kaye was dozing in the passenger seat. It was quiet. And then I heard something like a sniffle. I didn't pay any attention to it because when you have three small children someone is always sniffling.

There it was again—the sniffle. Only louder this time. I ignored it, thinking about the short time I had to sleep and the money I had spent.

Not a sniffle this time. A sob. It was Kim. I figured it was one of the hotdogs finally hitting bottom.

Louder now. Almost crying.

I said over my shoulder, "Honey, what's the matter?"

A sniffle, a sob, a tiny voice. "I didn't get a balloon."

Five hours to sleep, a hundred . . . "What was that, hon?"

"I said, I didn't get a balloon."

"What?"

"I didn't get a balloon. You promised I could get a balloon."

She was right, of course. When we went in that morning there was a man at the entrance selling balloons. Kim wanted one, but I told her she would have to hang on to it all day and would probably lose it. Wait until we leave, and I'll buy you one then, I said. But when we left I didn't see the balloon man, didn't even remember about the balloons. And, obviously, Kim hadn't either.

Now, I must remind you, this was years ago when I was younger and not the spiritually mature person I am now. Because I lost it.

I hit the brakes, pulled the car over on the shoulder, jammed the gear shift into park, and jerked around and said, "What did you say?"

"I didn't get a balloon. You said I could have a balloon. . . ."

"Listen," I said, as her two brothers became alert. "I have spent all day at Six Flags. I spent over a hundred dollars. I've got to get up in five hours to go to church—and all you can say is you didn't get a balloon!

"I didn't hear one of you say, 'Thank you, Dad. Thanks, Dad, for taking all day Saturday; thanks for spending a hundred dollars; thanks for the rides and the hotdogs.'"

And I was right.

"I did all that, and the only thing you mention is the silly balloon you didn't get!"

By this time Kaye was awake and patting me on the leg, telling me it was all right.

And it was, I guess. But, doggone, you do all that for your children, and the only thing they remember is the one thing they didn't get.

I guess that's why we call them children.

Part Five: Getting the Best Out of the Worst—
The Ministry of Circumstance

God judged it better to bring good out of evil than to suffer
no evil to exist.

> Augustine

As the wicked are hurt by the best things, so the godly are
bettered by the worst.

> William Jenkyn

All I have seen teaches me to trust the Creator for all I have
not seen.

> Ralph Waldo Emerson

22

THE MOST UNBELIEVABLE VERSE IN THE BIBLE

And we know that God causes all things to work together for good to those who love God, to those who are called according to His purpose.

Romans 8:28, NAS

I've been looking for loopholes in this verse.

I've read all the liberal commentaries, compared all the translations, studied the sentence structure and word definitions in the Greek—in an effort to find something wrong with it. In short, to prove that it doesn't really say what it seems to say. This is the verse I preached from three days after we buried our son. I had preached it plenty of times before, but that didn't seem to count anymore. I've always believed that you don't have a right to shout "Praise the Lord" at a funeral unless it is your loved one in the casket; I figured the same principle applied here. It was fairly easy to preach the sermon that Friday night in Kansas City.

But it has not always been easy since. When you experience a great tragedy, you may feel you've paid your dues and that's the end of it. But I found that the dues are never paid up—or so it seems. Ronnie, Jr.'s death was only the first of many deaths, not physical deaths like his, of course, but deaths just as real that brought grief just as painful.

And so I got real serious about this verse, which promises too much to be true. For Paul seems to be saying that if we love God and are called according to His purpose, *all things*, not some things or even most things, but all things are working together for our good. "We know," Paul says, and he uses the word for certainty. This isn't guess work, the apostle tells us. We know with absolute certainty that this is so.

WHAT IT DOESN'T MEAN

The greatest danger in dealing with this verse is romanticizing it, oversimplifying it, taking the sting out of the preceding verses about suffering.

Paul is not saying that whatever happens to a Christian is good. A lot of bad things happen to us. We cannot say that what happens is best. But it will be worked out for our good, the best. The bad things that happen to us have no weight in thwarting the good God intends for us.[1]

Paul doesn't mean that God works out all things for our comfort, convenience, health, and wealth. These "things" of which Paul speaks do not serve the worldly interests of the believer. Whatever "good" Paul has in mind has to do with our salvation and our relationship to the God who has saved us.

Neither is Paul saying that everything in life will work out for the best, as though things will work themselves out. Things do not work out for good. *God* works things out for good. He oversees our life and is active in our day-by-day experience. And this is done only for those "who love God." For the unsaved, nothing ultimately, in eternity, works out for their good.

A CLOSER LOOK

The context of this verse is important. The primary reference to "all things" is the "sufferings of this time" in verse 18: "For I consider that the sufferings of this present time are not worthy to be compared with the glory that is to be revealed to us" (Rom. 8:18, NAS).

Romans 8:28 not only looks back to verse 18, but it looks forward to verses 35–39 as well:

"Who shall separate us from the love of Christ? Shall tribulation, or distress, or persecution, or famine, or nakedness, or peril, or sword? . . .

But in all these things we overwhelmingly conquer through Him who loved us. For I am convinced that neither death, nor life, nor angels, nor principalities, nor things present, nor things to come, nor powers, nor height, nor depth, nor any other created thing [just in case he missed something], shall be able to separate us from the love of God, which is in Christ Jesus our Lord." (NAS)

Do you see my problem? Paul appears to be saying that *all things*, even things like persecution and death and famine and distress, are used to profit those who love God. He claims, or so it seems, that in God's government of this world, God sees to it that all things contribute to the welfare of His people.

C. E. B. Cranfield, in his highly acclaimed commentary on Romans, says, "We understand the first part of the verse, then, to mean that nothing can really harm—that is,

185

harm in the deepest sense of the word—those who really love God, but that all things which may happen to them, including such grievous things as are mentioned in v. 35, must serve to help them on their way to salvation, confirming their faith and drawing them closer to their Master, Jesus Christ. But the reason why all things thus assist believers is, of course that God is in control of all things. *The faith expressed here is faith not in things but in God."* [2]

God's power and authority are such that even the actions of the enemies of God and His people must subserve His will.[3]

If this is true, it means that my complaints against life and God, no matter how understandable, are not legitimate.

If this is true, it means that I have no right to cling to anger or to harbor bitterness against whatever injustices I may have suffered.

If this is true, it means that the pain Kaye and I encountered a few weeks ago when we buried a cherished dream—even that is destined for our good.

If this is true, it means that if God subtracted one pain, one heartache, one disappointment from my life, I would be less than the person I am now, less than the person God wants me to be, and my ministry would be less than He intends.

If this is true, it means that I can climb over those hurts and disappointments, over the tears and heartaches, over the graves and sleepless nights, and stand on top of that ash-heap and declare, "All these things God is working together for my good."

As I write I am surrounded by stacks of commentaries on the book of Romans, the latest and the greatest, and by piles of papers and notes I have searched through a hundred times—and I must tell you—I have found no loophole.

CHAPTER
23

DOES MY LIFE MAKE ANY SENSE?

I am haunted by a newspaper story. It told of a young secretary who, one day during her lunch hour, climbed out on the ledge of the building in which she was working and announced her intentions to jump. Life, at least hers, had no purpose, made no sense, and she was going to end it.

The police were called, the fire department, the psychologists and counselors, but when they tried to talk to her, she threatened to jump.

Finally, she agreed to talk to a minister. He sat on the window sill just a few unreachable feet from the girl and spoke to her for two hours. At the end of those two hours, she jumped to her death.

I wonder what they talked about. What did he say to her? I wonder if he has nightmares.

But what haunts me about that story is, What would *I* have said to her? What would you have said?

Does life make any sense? Albert Camus, the French existentialist, said that the only serious philosophical question is the question of suicide.[1]

The Bible's answer to that is, YES! Life does make sense; it is worth living: "And we know that all things work for the good of those who love him, who have been called according to his purpose."

What beautiful, life-affirming words: "All things work for the good. . . ."

But there is a limitation to this promise of Romans 8:28—it is to those who love God, to those who are called according to His purpose. "Called to his purpose" further defines "those who love God." Those who love God are those called according to His purpose.

SUFFERING: RADICAL OR REDEMPTIVE?

In the earlier section on Job, I used the terms "radical suffering" and "tragedy" to describe suffering that dehumanizes a person because it is undeserved and without purpose, other than to degrade the sufferer (the Nazi death camps leap to mind).

But the suffering of which Paul speaks in the eighth chapter of Romans is *redemptive*, not radical.

It is redemptive because God causes it to fit into His purpose. This is a redemption-centered universe. God governs the universe for a redemptive purpose—consummated redemption—glorification—one far-off divine event toward which the whole creation moves.[2]

In other words, God has designed a purpose for us, and even evil and suffering are made to promote that purpose. I'm not saying that God causes the evil and the suffering, but when it occurs, God works it to our ultimate advantage—His purpose.

When the Bible says that all things work together for our good, it means that all things work together to accomplish

God's purpose. God's purpose is the good; the good is God's purpose.

SO WHAT IS THAT PURPOSE?

Paul tells us in the next verse: "For whom He foreknew, He also predestined to become conformed to the image of His Son" (Rom. 8:29, NAS). Or as the William translation reads, "He marked them off to be like His Son."[3] The purpose of God is to make us like Jesus.

Humans were created in the image of God. That means that of all God's creatures, only humans were made with the capacity to know God and enjoy fellowship with Him. As the catechism reminds us: "The chief end of man is to glorify God and enjoy Him forever."

When the first man sinned he did not lose that image; it was marred but not destroyed. The TV news the other night reported the fierce fighting in Bosnia. They showed picture after picture of bombed-out buildings. Some walls were still standing, enough that you could tell what they were. They were no longer habitable, but they still had some semblance of what they were originally.

When Adam fell in the Garden of Eden, it was as though a bomb exploded, not destroying the image of God, but marring it. And with the marring of God's image in man, everything in man's life was marred—especially his relationship with God. Now, to be sure, there is still within us the capacity to know Him and the desire to fellowship with Him. But it has been crippled. In salvation, God intends to restore that image.

THE IMAGE OF GOD/THE IMAGE OF HIS SON

Have you noticed that Paul does not say we are being conformed to the image of God, but rather to the image of His Son? And this is the emphasis throughout the New Testament.

Christ came not only to show us what the Father is like, but also to reveal what man, true man, unfallen man, is supposed to be—to show us what it means to glorify God and enjoy Him forever. He is the God-man, the perfect example of what a person's relationship with God should be. In His humanity, Christ suffered loneliness, misunderstanding, hunger, thirst, abandonment, and death, the pain and humiliation of which defy description. Yet He remained in perfect fellowship with His Father and His brethren. Suffering was a part of His image; by it He was made perfect. And in that humanity and fellowship with the Father, the glory of God blazed through. Jesus was what God purposed man to be and what we will be. We who have been called according to His purpose will be transformed into the likeness of the inner character of Christ.

A FUTURE FULFILLMENT

This purpose will be realized in every one of us. I immediately think of that great passage in 1 Corinthians 15, where Paul says, "And just as we have borne the likeness of the earthly man, so shall we bear the likeness of the man from heaven. . . . Listen, I tell you a mystery: We will not all sleep, but we will all be changed—in a flash, in the twinkling of an eye, at the last trumpet. For the trumpet will sound, the dead will be raised imperishable, and we will be changed. For the perishable must clothe itself with the imperishable, and the mortal with immortality" (vv. 49–53).

And then the words of John: "Dear friends, now we are children of God, and what we will be has not yet been made known. But we know that when he appears, we shall be like him, for we shall see him as he is" (1 John 3:2).

Paul told the Philippians that he was confident "that he who began a good work in you will carry it on to completion until the day of Christ Jesus" (1:6).

God always finishes what He starts. He did not rest on the seventh day until He completed the six days of creation. The writer of Hebrews says of Jesus, "After he had provided purification for sins, he sat down at the right hand of the Majesty in heaven."

A PRESENT PROCESS

While the actual fulfillment of this promise lies in the future, it is a process that is already taking place. Paul said that God, who had begun the good work in us, would carry it on to completion. *Completion.* You can't complete something until you have started it. Let's go back to the passage in 1 John, where the apostle tells us that when Jesus appears we will be like Him, for we shall see Him as He is. Verse 3 makes this statement: "Everyone who has this hope in him purifies himself, just as he is pure."

Are you familiar with Paul's words in 2 Corinthians 3:18? "And we, who with unveiled faces all reflect the Lord's glory, are being transformed into his likeness with ever-increasing glory, which comes from the Lord, who is the Spirit." The alternate reading for "reflect" is "contemplate." As we *contemplate* the glory of the Lord, we are being changed into the same image.

God is saying that one of these days, somewhere down the road, we will hear a shout and the sound of a trumpet, and in a flash we will be changed into the likeness of our Lord. In the meantime, see how far down the road you can get. That way, the change, when it comes, won't be such a trauma for you. Some talk of the coming of Christ as a rapture, but I think for many it will be a rupture because we will be so unlike Jesus.

It is at this point that Romans 8:28 begins to make sense. Even now, in this present life with all its afflictions, if I have that hope within me, the "all things" can serve to refine me and shape me so that I will that much more resemble my Savior.

It is through the "all things" of our earthly experience that God works into us a Christ-like compassion for those who hurt and a Christ-like love for our enemies and a Christ-like submission to the Father's will.

Do you know this story? A man visited the studio of a sculptor, and in the middle of the room sat a huge slab of marble.

"What are you going to sculpt out of that marble?" the man asked.

"A horse," answered the sculptor.

"How will you do that?" the visitor asked.

"I will take a hammer and a chisel and knock off everything that doesn't look like a horse."

I think it is fair to say that God's purpose is to knock off of us everything that doesn't look like Jesus.

24

PROVIDENCE AND A GUY NAMED JOE

I began this book with Jacob, presenting him as a paradigm of God's dealings with His people—"a struggle till the breaking of day." I close the book with Joseph and Romans 8:28 as a summary of all I have said about God's silence and His strange ministers.

With Joseph, God was silent for twenty-five years. And he had his share of strange ministers: his brothers, the Midianites, the Ishmaelites, Potiphar, Potiphar's wife, the butler and the baker, Pharaoh, famine. But God worked it all together for good.

PROVIDENCE

The purpose of God is to conform us to the image of God's Son. It is the providence of God that accomplishes that purpose in our daily lives.

You may be thinking, "I see the word *purpose* in that passage, but I don't see the word *providence*." You're right, the word isn't there. But it is there—in verse 28: "And we know that God causes all things to work together for good. . . ." *Providence* is all things working together.

Providence comes from two words—*pro*, meaning "before," and *video*, meaning "to see." To see before is providence. The providence of God means that God sees beforehand and plans accordingly.

We exercise providence every day. I have a pack of Rolaids in my pocket right now; I know I'll probably have heartburn before the day is over. I also carry sinus medicine with me because I have a sinus headache nearly every day. Do you have life insurance? That's providence. You have seen ahead and have planned accordingly, so that when the time comes, provision will have already been made.

God sees beforehand everything that's going to happen in my life. "Oh, Dunn's going to run into trouble there. I'll go ahead and prepare things so that when he hits that tough spot, it will fit into My purpose for him." That's providence. It is God seeing ahead of time what is going to happen and planning accordingly so that when it happens it will fit into His plan.

A GUY NAMED JOE

A great picture of providence is found in the life of Joseph, a boy loved by his father and loathed by his brothers (Gen. 37–50). He was his father's favorite because he had been born to Jacob in his old age, and he was the firstborn son of Rachel, Jacob's favorite wife.

He was loathed by his brothers because he *was* the favorite and Jacob doted on him. But Joseph was also a tattletale, reporting to his father whenever his brothers did something wrong.

Probably the thing that grated on his brothers the most were the dreams Joseph had in which he saw his ten older brothers bowing down before him. Now this may not seem like a big deal to us, but in that culture it was intolerable and unheard of. Of course, there was nothing wrong with Joseph having the dreams, but he didn't have to rub it in by repeating them to his brothers.

One day, wearing the new brightly colored sport coat his father had given him (something else he could taunt his brothers about), Joseph was sent to check up on his brothers. He found them in Dothan. When they saw him coming, they said, "Here comes that dreamer. Let's kill him! Then let's see what becomes of his dreams!" (see Gen. 37:1–20).

But Reuben persuaded them not to kill the boy; just throw him in a pit in the wilderness and let him die.

After throwing him in a pit, they had lunch. As they were eating, they saw a caravan of Ishmaelites heading their way. They said, "We can make some money off this deal. Let's pull Joseph out of the pit and sell him to those guys."

That's bad. Well, not so bad, because before they reached the pit, some Midianites traders happened by, saw Joseph in the pit, and pulled him out.

That's good. Well, not so good, because they sold him to the Ishmaelites, who dragged him to Egypt, where Jews weren't appreciated, and sold him as a slave.

That's bad. Well, not so bad, because they sold him to Potiphar, one of Pharaoh's officers, who did not hate the Jews.

That's good. Well, not so good, because Potiphar's wife began to hit on Joseph and tried to seduce him.

That's bad. Well, not so bad, because Joseph refused her advances.

That's good. Well, not so good, because she lied and said that Joseph tried to rape her, and he was thrown in prison.

That's bad. Well, not so bad, because in prison he met a chief cupbearer and a chief baker who, because Joseph was able to interpret their dreams, vowed they would remember him when they were released.

That's good. Well, not so good, because they forgot about him. At least the cupbearer did; the baker was hanged.

But then Pharaoh himself began to be troubled by his dreams and could find no one to tell him what they meant. Suddenly the cupbearer remembered his former cellmate's ability to explain dreams. Joseph was brought before Pharaoh and interpreted the monarch's dreams—which said that there were going to be seven years of fatness, then seven years of famine.

On the spot Pharaoh appointed Joseph as food administrator, gave him the king's signet ring, dressed him in fine clothes, and placed a gold chain around his neck. He put Joseph in charge of the palace, and his entire household were told to submit to Joseph's orders.

And if that wasn't enough, listen to what the king said, "I am Pharaoh, but without your word no one will lift hand or foot in all Egypt" (Gen. 41:44).

Providence. God saw ahead and made plans so that when Joseph's brothers cast him into the pit, it would fit into His purpose. He had that caravan pass by at just the right time. Do you realize all those camels had to be born at just the right moment for it to happen as it did? Every step of the way God went before Joseph, anticipating each problem and making it serve His will.

A FAMILY REUNION

After seven years of fatness came the seven years of famine, as Joseph had said. First, the Egyptians came to Joseph for food, and eventually the other nations did also.

Then one day, Joseph's brothers showed up, seeking food. They didn't recognize their little brother, of course. It had been twenty-five years since they threw him in the pit. But Joseph recognized them. At first, he kept his identity a secret, but eventually he could bear it no longer and, weeping, told them who he was.

Understandably, the brothers were terrified. This was not good news. Joseph would surely have them slain. They came seeking food, and all they were going to get was the sharp edge of a sword.

But Joseph said, "Do not be angry with yourselves for selling me here, *because it was to save lives that God sent me ahead of you*" (Gen. 45:5, italics added).

And again, he said: "*But God sent* me ahead of you to preserve for you a remnant on earth and to save your lives by a great deliverance" (Gen. 45:7, italics added).

And again, "So then, *it was not you who sent me here, but God*. He made me father to Pharaoh, lord of his entire household and ruler of all Egypt" (Gen. 45:8, italics added).

Three times Joseph says, "It was not you, but God who sent me here."

You say that it *was* his brothers and the slave traders that brought him to Egypt? You're entitled to your opinion, of course, but Joseph was there. He ought to know.

After the great reconciliation, Jacob, the father, is brought to Egypt, and once again the whole family is together.

197

But comes the day of Jacob's death, and the brothers say, "What if Joseph holds a grudge against us and pays us back for all the wrongs we did to him?"

When Joseph heard their fears, he broke down and wept, saying, "Don't be afraid. Am I in the place of God? *You intended to harm me, but God intended it for good* to accomplish what is now being done, the saving of many lives" (Gen. 50:19–20, italics added).

EVIL IN THE SERVICE OF GOOD

Do you realize that the brothers themselves brought about the fulfillment of Joseph's dreams, which they hated? If they had not thrown him in the pit, they would never have bowed before him in Egypt.

But a more fantastic thought: If those brothers had not done what they did, twenty-five years later they would have starved to death. And so would have Egypt and the other nations.

You could say that their sin became their salvation.

A LITTLE HOMEWORK

I have some homework for you. Get two sheets of paper and number 1 to whatever down the side of each sheet. Then on one sheet, list all the things in your life you feel you got a bum deal on. Maybe you were born into a broken home or in deep poverty or with a handicapping condition or with big ears.

On the other sheet, list all the things in your life right now that you would change if you could, but can't.

When you complete the two lists, start at the top of each sheet, read off each item, and say, "You meant it for evil, but God meant it for good."

What will that do for you? I don't know. But it helped change my life.

EPILOGUE

"I MAY BE DUNN, BUT I'M NOT FINISHED"

I am writing these final pages at Cape Cod. Kaye and I come here every year around Labor Day as the guests of dear Christian friends. It seems fitting that I should finish the book here, because it was on our first trip to Cape Cod in 1986 that the darkness began to lift.

It was our thirtieth wedding anniversary. Usually, we celebrate by going to a fancy hotel, eating in a swank restaurant, and catching a couple of movies.

"Where do you want to go for our anniversary this year?" I asked casually.

"I want to go to Cape Cod," she answered, not at all casually.

Ask a question . . . Kaye is a hopeless romantic.

So the day after Labor Day, we threw some clothes in my little car, and without making a reservation anywhere, we took off for Cape Cod.

The best I can remember, it was when we crossed the Texas state line into Arkansas (this may or may not be significant), that I suddenly felt an extraordinary release as a decade of darkness fled my spirit. I gave a loud yelp and scared Kaye to death. She thought, *Oh God, he's finally gone over the edge.*

"Honey," I said. "Everything on this trip is going to be perfect. This is a gift from God."

And it was.

That's why we return every year at this time.

I don't mean that I have had no battles with the darkness since then. To the contrary. It has been a year and a half since I first sat down to write this book. In many ways it has been one of our most difficult times. The crisis I mentioned at the beginning was resolved—but not the way we wanted and not the way we prayed. In that time we have lost someone very dear to us, we have buried some dreams and given up some hopes, and we have been forced to close some important chapters in our lives.

But it has been good and bad running on parallel tracks.

It is a struggle until the breaking of day. *But the day will break.*

One of the blessings of having battled depression so often is that I have learned that I can defeat it.

I took a break from writing this morning to go fishing in Robert Fulghum's new pond, *Maybe (Maybe Not)*. I caught a beauty.

In one chapter Fulghum reveals his own desperate battle with depression and the urge of self-destruction. Speaking of this "dark, dangerous demon of death," that runs loose in his mind from time to time, Fulghum likens his triumph over this beast to that of a matador over the bull.

He is confident, he says, in the presence of this bull of self-destruction.

> This confidence is called *ver llegar* in the ring. It means "to watch them come." It is the ability to plant your feet exactly

so—to hold your ground and see calmly, as in slow motion, the charge of the bull, knowing that you have what it takes to maneuver the bull safely by. . . . It is confidence that comes from many passes and many fights—you can control the bull and defeat it because you have done it before. . . .

I know him now. I can smell him, sense him before he moves. I welcome him. Yah, Toro, come on. I plant my feet and watch him come. He charges. I pass him safely by with a swing of the cape of my confidence. The crowd in my head roars. OLÉ! The crowd is made up of all those ancestors who passed their bulls—they are pulling for me. OLÉ! OLÉ! OLÉ!"[1]

I, too, am confident in the presence of my bull. But my confidence lies not in my ability or experience. My confidence lies in Him who loved me and gave Himself for me.

> His love in times past
> Forbids me to think,
> He will leave me at last
> In trouble to sink.

I am always reluctant to finish a manuscript and mail it off.

In his preface to *Don Quixotes*, Cervantes says, "He that publishes a book runs a very great hazard, since nothing can be more impossible than to compose one that may secure the approbation of every reader."

I am especially reluctant to let this one go because it has become so personal. I didn't intend it to be that way, but books, like mischievous children, have a mind of their own and often run off in their own direction. But I agree with Henri Nouwen, who says that the thing that is most personal is most universal.[2] At the core of our being, down in the guts of our soul, we are all alike, fearing the same fears and desiring the same desires.

I am not an exception.
Neither are you.
That's the truth.
Honest.
I promise.

ENDNOTES

Chapter Three

1. John L. Maes, *Suffering: A Caregiver's Guide* (Nashville: Abingdon Press, 1990), p. 10.
2. *The Penguin Dictionary of Psychology*, compiled by James Drever, revised by Harvey Wallerstein (New York: Penguin Books, 1982 ed.), pp. 71, 72.
3. Walter Wink, *Engaging the Powers* (Minneapolis: Fortress Press, 1992), p. 94.

Chapter Four

1. Paul Tournier, *The Healing of Persons* (San Francisco: Harper & Row, 1965), p. 8.

Chapter Five

1. Elie Wiesel, *Messengers of God* (New York: Summit Books, 1976), p. 124.
2. Paul Tillich, *The Eternal Now* (New York: Charles Scribner's Sons, 1963), p. 103.

Chapter Six

1. Douglas John Hall, *God and Human Suffering* (Minneapolis: Augsburg Publishing House, 1986), p. 105.
2. *Ibid.*, p. 106.
3. *Ibid.*, p. 107.

4. Viktor E. Frankl, *Man's Search for Meaning*; revised and updated (New York: Washington Square Press, 1985), p. 172.

Chapter Seven
1. Lewis B. Smedes, *A Pretty Good Person* (San Francisco: Harper & Row, 1990), p. 20.
2. Virginia Stem Owens, "The Dark Side of Grace," *Christianity Today*, July 19, 1993, pp. 32–35.
3. *Ibid.*, p. 35.
4. *Ibid.*

Chapter Eight
1. Albert Camus, *The Myth of Sisyphus* (New York: Vintage Books, 1955), p. 20.
2. Helmut Thielicke, *A Thielicke Trilogy* (Grand Rapids: Baker Book House, 1980), p. 209.
3. Jory Graham, "Anger as Freedom," *To Provide Safe Passage*, ed. David and Pauline Rabin (New York: Philosophical Library, 1985), p. 70.
4. C. S. Lewis, *The Problem of Pain* (New York: Macmillan, 1962), pp. 14, 15.

Chapter Nine
1. Sue Chance, *Stronger Than Death* (New York: W.W. Norton & Company, 1992), p. 50.
2. G. Tom Milazzo, *The Protest and the Silence* (Minneapolis: Fortress Press, 1992), p. 43.
3. William A. Miller, *When Going to Pieces Holds You Together* (Minneapolis: Augsburg Publishing House, 1976), pp. 79, 80.
4. James L. Crenshaw, "Introduction: The Shift from Theodicy to Anthropodicy," in *Theodicy of the Old*

Testament, ed. James L. Crenshaw (Philadelphia: Fortress Press, 1983), p. 2.

5. Ernest Becker, *Escape from Evil* (New York: The Free Press, 1975), p. 7.

6. Helmut Thielicke, *How the World Began,* trans. John W. Doberstein (Philadephia: Muhlenburg Press, 1961), p. 171.

7. Warren W. Wiersbe, *Why Us?* (Old Tappan: Fleming H. Revell Company, 1984), p. 46.

8. Richard M. Zaner, "A Philosopher Reflects: A Play Against Night's Advance," in *To Provide Safe Passage,* ed. David and Pauline Rabin (New York: Philosophical Library, 1985), p. 241.

9. M. Scott Peck, *People of the Lie* (New York: Simon and Schuster, 1983), p. 41.

10. Crenshaw, *op. cit.*, p. 3.

11. *Ibid.*, p. 1.

12. Kornelis Miskotte, *When the Gods Are Silent* (New York: Harper & Row, 1967), pp. 252, 253.

13. Gabriel Marcel, *Being and Having*, trans. by Kathryn Farrer (London: Dacre Press/Westminister, 1949), p. 143.

Chapter Ten

1. C. S. Lewis, *A Grief Observed*, (New York: Bantam, 1976), pp. 4, 5.

2. Quoted by Wiersbe, *op. cit.*, p. 51.

3. Leon Morris, *The New International Commentary, the Gospel of John*, (Grand Rapids: Wm. B. Eerdmans Publishing Co., 1971), p. 477, footnote 5.

4. George A. Turner and Julius R. Mantey, *The Gospel of John*, (Grand Rapids: Wm. B. Eerdmans Publishing Co., n.d.), p. 202, footnote 1.

5. B. F. Westcott, *The Gospel According to St. John* (Grand Rapids: Wm. B. Eerdmans Publishing Co., n.d.), p. 144.
6. Philip Yancey, *Where Is God When It Hurts?* (Grand Rapids: Zondervan Publishing House, 1977), p. 97.
7. Jan Cox-Gedmark, *Coping with Physical Disability* (Philadelphia: The Westminster Press, 1980), p. 40.
8. Hans Küng, *Does God Exist?* (New York: Vintage Books, 1981), p. 674.
9. Richard M. Zaner, "A Philosopher Reflects: A Play Against Night's Advance," in *To Provide Safe Passage*, David and Pauline Rabin, ed. (New York: Philosophical Library, 1985), p. 241.
10. Helmut Thielicke, *A Thielicke Trilogy* (Grand Rapids: Baker Book House, 1980), pp. 210, 211.
11. Jory Graham, "Anger as Freedom," in *To Provide Safe Passage*, p. 75.

Chapter Eleven

1. R. Laird Harris, Gleason L. Archer, Jr., Bruce K. Waltke, *Theological Wordbook of the Old Testament*, Vol. 1 (Chicago: Moody Press, 1980), p. 303.
2. W. Lee Humphreys, *The Tragic Vision and the Hebrew Tradition* (Philadelphia: Fortress Press, 1985), p. 95.
3. *Ibid.*, p. 96.

Chapter Twelve

1. H. Wheeler Robinson, *The Cross in the Old Testament* (Philadelphia: The Westminister Press, 1955), p. 45.
2. John D. Barbour, *Tragedy as a Critique of Virtue* (Chico, CA: Scholars Press, 1984), p. ix.
3. Wendy Farley, *Tragic Vision and Divine Compassion: A Contemporary Theodicy* (Louisville: Westminister/John Knox Press, 1990), p. 12.

4. Michael J. Buckley, S.J. *At the Origins of Modern Atheism* (New Haven: Yale University Press, 1987), p. 328.

Chapter Thirteen

1. Diana and Lisa Berger, *We Heard the Angels of Madness* (New York: William Morrow and Company, Inc., 1991), p. 185.
2. Humphreys, *op. cit.*, p. 105.
3. *Ibid.*, emphasis added. p. 115.
4. Cynthia Swindoll quoted in Don Baker, *Depression: Finding Hope & Meaning in Life's Darkest Shadow* (Portland, Or: Multnomah Press, 1983), p. 5.
5. Maes, *op. cit.*, p. 20.
6. James L. Crenshaw, *A Whirlpool of Torment: Israelite Traditions of God as an Oppressive Presence* (Philadelphia: Fortress Press, 1984), pp. 59, 60, 61, 63.
7. *Ibid.*, p. 59.
8. C. S. Lewis, *A Grief Observed* (New York: Bantam Books, 1976), p. 5.

Chapter Fourteen

1. H. Wheeler Robinson, *The Cross in the Old Testament* (Philadelphia: The Westminister Press, 1955), p. 47.
2. Humphreys, *op. cit.*, p. 120.

Chapter Fifteen

1. Richard Foster, *Prayer: Finding the Heart's True Home* (San Francisco: HarperCollins, 1992), p. 18.
2. *Ibid.*, p. 18.
3. Martin Marty, *A Cry of Absence* (San Francisco: Harper & Row Publishers, 1983), p. 2.
4. *Ibid.*, pp. 2, 3.
5. *Ibid.*, p.5, emphasis added.

6. Dorothee Sölle, *Suffering* (Philadelphia: Fortress Press, 1975), p. 76.
7. Samuel Balentine, *The Hidden God* (Oxford: Oxford University Press, 1982), p. 172.
8. Walter Brueggemann, *The Message of the Psalms* (Minneapolis: Augsburg Publishing House, 1984), p. 80.
9. *Ibid.*, p. 80.
10. *Ibid.*, pp. 51, 52.
11. *Ibid.*, p. 52.

Chapter Sixteen
1. William Styron, *Darkness Visible: A Memoir of Madness* (New York: Random House, 1990), p. 7.
2. Grace Ketterman, *Depression Hits Every Family* (Nashville: Oliver Nelson, 1988), pp. 16–19.
3. John White, *The Masks of Melancholy* (Downer's Grove: InterVarsity Press, 1982), p. 77.
4. For more information about Rapha, call toll free (24-hour) 1–800–227–2657 or the minister's hotline, 1–800–383–HOPE, or write Rapha, 8876 Gulf Freeway, Suite 340, Houston, TX 77017.
5. J. Christian Beker, *Suffering and Hope* (Philadelphia: Fortress Press, 1987), p. 9.
6. Styron, *op. cit.*, p. 38.
7. *Ibid.*, p. 50.
8. Thomas Moore, *Care of the Soul* (San Francisco: HarperCollins Publishers, 1992), pp. 137, 138.

Chapter Seventeen
1. Lewis, *A Grief Observed*, p. 34.
2. Manuel de Unamuno, *The Private World* (Princeton: Princeton University Press, 1984), p. 44.

3. Oswald Chambers, *My Utmost for His Highest* (New York: Dodd, Mead andCompany, 1935), p. 305.
4. Quoted by Philip Yancey, *Disappointment with God* (Grand Rapids: Zondervan Publishing House, 1988), p. 17.

Chapter Eighteen

1. John Irving, *A Prayer for Owen Meany* (New York: Ballantine Books, 1989), p. 44.
2. Gary Collins, *The Magnificent Mind* (Waco: Word Books, 1985), pp. 147, 148.

Chapter Nineteen

1. I have written about knowing God's will in *Don't Just Stand There, Pray Something*, Thomas Nelson Publishers, pp. 208–214.
2. J. I. Packer, *Hot Tub Religion*, (Wheaton: Tyndale House Publishers, 1987), p. 106.
3. John White, *The Fight* (Downers Grove: InterVarsity Press, 1978), p. 158.

Chapter Twenty

1. John White, *Parents in Pain* (Downers Grove: Inter-Varsity Press, 1979), p. 36.
2. Harold Kushner, *When All You've Ever Wanted Isn't Enough* (New York: Summit Books, 1986), pp. 150, 151.

Chapter Twenty-two

1. J. B. McBeth, *Exegetical and Practical Commentary on Romans* (Shawnee: Oklahoma Baptist University Press, 1937), p. 198.
2. C. E. B. Cranfield, *Critcal and Exegetical Commentary to Romans*, Vol. 1 (Edinburgh: Clark, 1975), p. 429, emphasis added.

3. *Ibid.*, p. 429.

Chapter Twenty-three
1. Camus, *op. cit.*, p. 3.
2. *op. cit.*, McBeth, p. 198.
3. *The New Testament in the Language of the People:* Charles B. Williams, copyright © 1937, 1965, 1966, 1986, published by Holman Bible Publishers.

Epilogue
1. Robert Fulghum, *Maybe (Maybe Not)* (New York: Villard Books, 1993), pp. 105, 106.
2. Henri J. M. Nouwen, *The Wounded Healer* (New York: Doubleday, 1972), p. 16.